GRANDPARENTING
WITH
LOVE & LOGIC

PRACTICAL SOLUTIONS TO
TODAY'S GRANDPARENTING
CHALLENGES

JIM FAY &
FOSTER W. CLINE, M.D.

The Love and Logic
PRESS, Inc.
2207 Jackson St.
Golden, CO 80401

ISBN 0-944634-54-0

Library of Congress Cataloging-in-Publication Data

Fay, Jim.
    Grandparenting with love and logic: practical solutions to today's grandparenting challenges / by Jim Fay and Foster W. Cline.
        p. cm.
    Includes bibliographical references and index.
    ISBN 0-944634-06-0 (hc)
    ISBN 0-944634-54-0 (pb)
    1. Grandparenting—United States. I. Cline, Foster W.
II. Title.
HQ759.9.9.F39 ,1994
306.874'5—dc20   94-38940
                                                              CIP

The actual text of *Grandparenting With Love and Logic* was written by Carol Von Klombenburg. Editing by Adryan Russ.
Designed by Bob Schram, Bookends.
Jacket design by Barry Eisenach, Phoenix Design.

Printed in the United States of America

Contents

PART TWO: *Love & Logic Pearls:*
Strategies and Situations for Specific Issues

Love and Logic Tips

Introduction

Children have changed since we, who used to be children, have grown into parents and grandparents. Parenting and grandparenting have changed, too. Across the country, experts studying these changes have made the following observations:

❖ Today's grandparents are younger, healthier, and more involved than ever before.[1]
❖ The changing structure of our population has resulted in a greater number of three- and four-generation families. As a result, an expanding position within the family is that of grandparent.[2]
❖ Grandparenting of the past cannot serve as a model for grandparenting today. The chance for large-scale restoration of traditional values is near zero—particularly as far as grandparents are concerned.[3]

Grandparents don't need experts to tell them about these changes. They know firsthand. As one grandmother said, "I was comparing my grandchild's upbringing to that of my own children, but it can't be done. This is a different day and age."

Why We've Written This Book

While helping parents across the country cope with our changing world, we began to realize there is another generation also hungry for help—grandparents. Our survey turned up a variety of books, some about historical and sociocultural changes in the family; others that approach grandparenting as if the stereotyped 1950s nuclear family were still the norm. We found few practical, usable techniques or solutions for today's grandparenting dilemmas and challenges—none at all that presented information grandparents could use immediately. That's when we decided to write this book.

For more than ten years, we've been providing practical help to parents at the Love and Logic Institute. Our books, *Parenting with Love and Logic,* and *Parenting Teens with Love and Logic* (Piñon Press), have been well received by more than a quarter of a million people.

Our goals are to:

❖ Help grandparents develop and nurture healthy, loving, enjoyable, and fulfilling relationships with their children and grandchildren.
❖ Give grandparents practical, usable skills and techniques that can enhance relationships and improve problem areas with their children and grandchildren—both short- and long-term.

❖ Provide grandparents with as much guidance as possible to help their grandchildren develop into responsible, caring young people.

How to Read This Book

We've divided this book into two parts:

Part I offers basic grandparenting techniques and principles to use in today's world, including those that apply when parents divorce and when grandparents find they have become their grandchild's parent. Chapters 1–5 are the foundation for the rest of the book and important for all grandparents. Chapters 6–10 present a variety of choices. We invite you to either read them all, or select those chapters most relevant to you and your situation. Chapter 11 revisits basic Love and Logic principles.

Part II is even more practical. It presents fortyone Pearls, that offer strategies for dealing with specific issues, such as gift-giving, playing favorites, baby-sitting, and the three-generation home. The Pearls are listed in the Contents for easy reference.

Love and Logic Is An Attitude

Grandparenting with Love and Logic is not a comprehensive system, but an attitude based on two principles:

Love: We give love—love that goes beyond permission, insists upon mutual respect, allows others their mistakes, and empathizes with the disappointment and pain that follow such mistakes.

Logic: We use logic—which recognizes and acknowledges that others must live with the consequences of their mistakes and, therefore, allows them time, with patience, to learn from the choices they've made.

Throughout, the book is sprinkled with Love and Logic Tips, which expand on these basic principles for grandparents—for any adults—in their relationships with children.

You don't often get second chances in life. Love and Logic can help you solve problems and enhance relationships with your grandchildren and your adult children. Grandparenting can be a parent's second chance—to give what you may have missed giving the first time around.

~PART ONE~

*Techniques & Principles
for Grandparenting
Today*

⫷ 1 ⫸

Love and Logic
for Grandparents

*The joys of parents are secret, and so are
their griefs and fears.*
—Francis Bacon
"Of Parents and Children"

T old as a folk tale, the Love and Logic story of
grandparenting would sound something like this:
Once upon a time, long before the creation of grandparents, there was the creation of parents. Parents were
designed in three basic styles: The helicopter. The drill
sergeant. The consultant. When parenting gave way to
grandparenting, those three varieties held fast, and they
are still around today.

Three Kinds of Grandparents

Helicopters. Some grandparents (as well as some parents) are helicopters. They hover, whirl their propellers,
and rotate their lives around their children and grandchildren. Although they don't travel very fast or get very
far, they create a lot of wind and racket. Helicopters are

easy to find. They are the ones hovering over the front yard, making sure the neighborhood bully isn't beating up on their child. They are the ones running back and forth to school each morning, carting forgotten lunches, permission slips, jackets, and warm-up suits.

These whirly-birds tend to whine. They say, "Why can't you ever remember your lunch?" "I really don't think I should have to remind you every morning." Or they complain: "I really would appreciate a little help. I get tired doing everything myself."

Grandparent helicopters, just as noisy as parent helicopters, swoop in to rescue both children and grandchildren at the first sign of trouble: "Can't find a sitter? I'll take the kids for you." Perhaps they've just taken a new job, or made a lunch date with a friend; but they give these up to go into child care.

Drill Sergeants. Similar to helicopters, drill sergeant grandparents make a lot of noise. But it's a different kind. They bark orders: "Put on your jacket before you leave this house!" "Put your lunch in your school bag!" "Take your permission slip!"

These order-givers know how to threaten by turning up the volume: "When will you *ever* learn to hang up your coat!" "When am I going to see the day I don't have to *remind* you to help me?"

Drill sergeant grandparents are just as tough as their children, who learned everything they know about drill sergeanting from them. They may use a softer tone of voice, but they still give orders: "The way to get that kid to stop bedwetting is, tell him he can't do it. He'll keep doing it as long as he knows he can get away with it."

Consultants. Some grandparents are consultants. When their children or grandchildren call home from school about forgotten lunches, they sympathize: "That's too bad. You might get really hungry by this afternoon. Good thing a big supper is planned tonight. Hang in there!"

They ask, "Do you plan to wear your coat today?" They leave the decision up to the child, who has already checked the thermometer hanging outside the kitchen window.

Consultants listen and provide choices. "You can't find a sitter? That must be frustrating. I'd be willing to help one day a week. I'm free on either Tuesday or Thursday. Which works best for you?" Or: "Jimmy is still wetting the bed? That must be difficult for you. What are you considering doing about it?"

Consultant grandparents don't whine or complain. They don't bark orders or stir up a lot of sound and fury, signifying nothing. To be a consultant is to grand-parent and parent with Love and Logic. And that's the style we believe is most effective.

Each grandparenting style sends a hidden message: Helicopters send the message that their children and grandchildren are helpless. Drill sergeants signal that their children and grandchildren cannot make their own decisions. Consultants beam loud and clear that they care about and encourage their children and grandchildren. Which message would you prefer to send? To honestly answer that question, ask yourself which message you would prefer to receive.

On the following page you will see a chart outlining, in a nutshell, the three varieties of parenting and grandparenting. Hopefully it will help you determine which style is going to work best for you. We know that the Love and Logic attitude works. We have seen it work across the country for thousands of parents. Now you will see how it can help you as a grandparent. We believe it will make your life a lot simpler—something we all welcome in today's world.

Three Basic Principles of Love and Logic

It's ironic that some of us have looked forward to our retirement as an oasis, a place to relax, with time on our hands; but in reality, now that we have arrived at these leisure years, we find no fistfuls of empty hours waiting to be frittered away. Many of us are still working, still parenting. The number of years we expect to spend on this earth seems to have increased since we were children. As a result, we continue to plan, to travel, to do.

Love and Logic can work for grandparents who are busy, because it is not a complicated system with a lot of do-and-don't rules to memorize. From all the materials we've studied on parenting and grandparenting, we have found three basic principles that run through all of them: 1) Set enforceable limits, 2) give people choices, and 3) allow consequences with empathy. Whenever you encounter a problem in your life as a grandparent, you can best find a solution by asking which principle makes the most sense for your situation.

As a foundation for these principles, it is imperative that you surround yourself with responsible people, people who have strong self-concepts. Until now, many experts have believed that building a positive self-concept has been important, but only as a side product of

HELICOPTERS

What they do:	• Rotate their lives around their children.
	• Run errands everyone else forgot to do.
	• Whirl, whine, and complain.
What they say:	• "Why can't you remember your lunch?"
	• "I'll take the kids while you work."
Their hidden message:	• You are helpless.
	• You are unable to handle the hurdles in your life, so I have to rescue you.

DRILL SERGEANTS

What they do:	• Bark out orders and call out their list.
	• Turn up the volume and threaten.
	• Command their troops to follow their instructions.
What they say:	• "Stand up straight."
	• "Don't leave without your warm jacket!"
	• "When will you ever learn?"
Their hidden message:	• I know better than you what's good for you.
	• You can't think for yourself.
	• Follow my orders and you'll be fine.

CONSULTANTS

What they do:	• Sympathize with the situation.
	• Listen and provide choices.
	• Leave the decision to the person with the problem.
What they say:	• "I'm sorry you've forgotten your lunch."
	• "Are you planning to wear a coat today?"
	• "I can baby-sit Tuesday or Thursday—which works best for you?"
Their hidden message:	• "I know you are strong and wise enough to handle the rocky sections of your life."
	• "I care about you and I'm here to encourage you while you travel this path."

healthy parenting. Today, we know better. A solid self-concept is essential in parenting and grandparenting, and, by simply using the three Love and Logic principles, you naturally help develop this self-concept in yourself, as well as in the people around you. Let's look at the principles in depth.

SET ENFORCEABLE LIMITS

With both grandchildren and adult children, it is crucial to set limits you can enforce. While it is difficult to enforce limits on someone else's behavior in an attempt to control that person, it is easy to set limits on your own behavior, once you know how.

❦ *Limit #1*
Only you know what you can do.
State what you are willing to do and what you plan to do.

Telling your child or grandchild how you plan to run your life is more workable than telling them how to run theirs. Nobody likes to be told what to do, in no uncertain terms, by someone else. Most people, however, will readily accept parameters you lay out for yourself. Listen to the difference between the following statements:

Unenforceable: "Why do you *always* expect me to be the baby-sitter? I have things I want to do, too, you know!"
Enforceable: "I can set aside four hours each week for baby-sitting, say, between 2:00 and 4:00 p.m., Tuesday through Saturday."

Unenforceable: "*You kids* should pick up after yourselves more often!"
Enforceable: "Dinner is served as soon as the toys are in the toy box."

❖ ❖ ❖

Unenforceable: "That kind of language won't be *tolerated* in this house!"
Enforceable: "You are welcome to visit whenever I don't have to listen to junior high street language."

❖ ❖ ❖

Unenforceable: "*Stop* that yelling!"
Enforceable: "I'll be glad to listen to you when your voice is at the same volume as mine."

❖ ❖ ❖

Unenforceable: "If you would just get a job on week-ends, you'd be able to afford college."
Enforceable: "I'm willing to provide $500 a year for each grandchild's college education."

❖ ❖ ❖

Unenforceable: "You should *always* wear a seatbelt!"
Enforceable: "You are invited to ride with me in the car as long as you wear your seatbelt."

When you set enforceable limits, be prepared for them to be tested. You may be met with potential fodder for disagreement:

❖ "That's not fair. My parents don't make me wear a seatbelt!"
❖ "If you really loved the grandchildren, you would want to see more of them!"

❖ "You can afford to fund full tuition, and you know it!"

When you are challenged in this way, all you need to remember is to simply acknowledge the opposing viewpoint by reaffirming your statement of limits. Then, imitate a broken record:

❖ "I know you feel it's not fair. And you're welcome to ride with me when you're wearing your seatbelt."

LOVE AND LOGIC TIP 1
Playing Broken Record

To avoid getting sidetracked by a child's protest or back-talk, an adult can play "broken record." The way to play is to repeat a statement or request kindly, without raising the voice, until the child verbally agrees to the request. Then the adult thanks the child for his or her cooperation.

Mike and Tom were hassling each other while watching TV. Their grandfather said, "Guys, you can hassle each other outdoors or you can watch TV quietly. It's up to you."

The hassling continued, so Grandpa said, "Guys, I'd like you to get up, turn off the TV, and play outside."

"We'll be quiet," they said.

"Guys, I'd like you to take it outside."

They tried a second protest. "The program is almost over."

"Take it outside, please, guys."

Mike tried again. "It's all Tom's fault."

"I'd like you to take it outside, please."

"Oh, all right, but that makes me mad, 'cause it's Tom's fault."

"I can hear that you're upset. Thanks for going outdoors."

Instead of getting sucked into a debate, Grandpa gently repeated his request. His "broken record" eventually led Mike and Tom to cooperate.

❖ "I know you believe I should see them more often. And I'll be glad to baby-sit four hours each week. Is between 2:00 and 4:00 p.m. good for you?"
❖ "I understand that you believe I can afford full tuition. What I am willing to provide is $500 per year per child."

🍎 *Limit #2*
Acknowledge the statement made by your adult child or grandchild; reaffirm your enforceable limit by repeating it.

To crumble when challenged is to throw your enforceable statement on the garbage heap. It weakens your self-concept and threatens to make your next enforceable statement even more difficult to maintain.

Besides setting workable limits, enforceable statements are useful in other ways. They help you take care of yourself in a loving way, which makes you an invaluable model for both younger generations. They will learn two essential lessons from you:

1. It's important to take good care of myself.

2. I am capable of handling my own problems. Although I may want to talk about them, I don't have to impose them on others.

Adult sons and daughters will learn it is their responsibility to find child care and financial alternatives. Grandchildren will learn it is their responsibility to put away their toys, and to obey the rules of the house or car they are in.

GIVE PEOPLE CHOICES

No one likes to be ordered around. Most people in this world have less control than they would like. People are happier when they have choices and prefer to be around others who share control through choices. So, if you are a grandparent, and you want to see more of your adult children and grandchildren, what do you suppose is the number one item you're going to want to offer them?

❦ *A grandparent's home can be a haven of coulds in a desert of shoulds.*

It is the wise grandparent who carefully offers choices he or she can live with.

Unwise choice: "You may play in the front yard or out in the street. What do *you* think?"
Wise choice: "You may play in the front yard or in the house. You decide."

Grandchildren enjoy being with you even more when they begin to understand that when they are with you, they get to make lots of decisions. As often as possible, you can offer a wealth of choices—scatter them freely during the course of the day—and accumulate a savings account of them. Then, when you need to cash in some chips, a withdrawal can be taken from the account:

Grandparent: "Aren't I pretty reasonable? Don't I let you make lots of decisions? Well, it's time for me to have a turn. Thanks for understanding."

LOVE AND LOGIC TIP 2
Choices or Demands?

Children, like all of us, respond better to choices than to demands. When we offer choices, the dynamics of an interaction change entirely. There are no demands to rebel against, and the control we need is established. Here's what choices do:

❖ *Create situations in which children must think over options, ponder courses of action, and make decisions.*
❖ *Provide opportunities for children to make mistakes and learn from consequences.*
❖ *Help parents and grandparents avoid control battles.*
❖ *Show children that we trust their thinking, which builds their self-confidence.*

If a grandchild dawdles over a meal and you have to be on the road in five minutes, you need not demand that he finish his burger in the next three minutes. You can offer him a choice: He can head out of the driveway with you, with burger finished or unfinished, feeling well fed or hungry.

Offering choices to grandchildren rather than making demands, actually gives you more control—and the beauty of it is that your relationship with them strengthens in the process.

The Expert Choice-Giver

One grandmother we know was an expert at giving choices. In the middle of her grandkids' favorite show, she asked if they wanted to go to bed then, or wait until the show was over. Do you need to ask which choice they made? When the show was over, she asked if they wanted a drink of kitchen water or bathroom water. In a glass or a cup? Straw or no straw? Walk to bed or ride piggyback? Story or no story? Door open or shut? Music or no music?

As she was leaving the room, with the light off and the music on, one of the children said, "Grandma, we love you. And couldn't we stay up just a little longer?"

Grandma took a withdrawal from her savings account. "You've had all the choices so far. Now I get to make one. Bedtime is now. Thanks for understanding—and I love you too."

The same pattern can be followed when taking grandchildren on an excursion. Will they wear their coats or carry them? Who will sit by the window on the way there, and who on the way back? Will you sing songs or not sing songs? Play card games or not play card games? Will they spend coins you give them on soft drinks, or on snacks? The cash-in comes when Grandpa decides what time the excursion ends. Grandpa says, "You've made all these decisions. Here's one I get to make. We need to leave here at 5:00 p.m. so we make it back home by 5:30, which is when Grandma is expecting us."

If the children object, Grandpa can say, "Wait a minute. Haven't I taken a back seat on all your decisions? Didn't you have a lot of choices today? Isn't it fair and square that I get a turn now?"

It's easier to gain cooperation from grandchildren who feel they have some measure of control—and actually do—than from those who have none.

Rita & Her Choices Business

One of our favorite stories comes from a grandmother named Rita who learned about choices decades ago. She used them constantly with her children and grandchildren. She knew Tammy, her three-year-old granddaughter, had caught on when Tammy came into the kitchen and asked, "Grandma, would you like me to have candy before dinner or after dinner?"

Recently, when Tammy and her mother were visiting for dinner, Rita asked her daughter after dessert, "Gina, would you like to wash or dry?"

Gina laughed and responded, "Nice try, Mom. That choices business used to work on me when I was a kid, but I'm onto your tricks now." In the meantime, Gina was absentmindedly clearing the table and loading the dishwasher!

Rita knew she had gone overboard the day she gave her cat two choices. But it's hard to overdo giving choices as long as you can live with the ones you offer, regardless of which one your grandchild or adult child picks.

When we give choices, we demonstrate that we are not control freaks. A grandfather, for example, with an adult son in need of transportation can offer, "I know you don't have a car and I know you need one. I can loan you mine for two half-days each week. Go ahead and decide which times would be best for you."

Our children and grandchildren enjoy being around us more when we share control. Grandparents, for example, wishing to see their grandchildren separately can say, "We'd like to see the grandchildren one-on-one during the month. You decide when each of the kids can come. We'd be glad to drive over for them."

There's no need to be a helicopter or drill sergeant, especially when you know the results you want come from being a caring consultant who understands who you are and your responsibility to that self.

ALLOW CONSEQUENCES WITH EMPATHY

The decisions we make in life that turn out to be mistakes are often followed by painful consequences. There are many responses we can offer our grandchildren and children experiencing these hard times. The most useful, however, is empathy. The best gift we can offer them is genuine sorrow and understanding.

Surviving the Cut

When Brad, not known as a self-starter in the work world, was laid off in the first round of cutbacks at his company, his father said, "That's rough, Brad. I've been afraid this would happen. If you want to survive cuts in the current economy, you've got to work 110 percent to make yourself indispensable."

A lecture from a drill sergeant was exactly what Brad did not need at that moment. A human brain can hold only one thing in its forefront at a time. Brad, who had just begun to mourn his own lack of motivation, instantly shifted gears and turned his remorse into anger.

"Dad," he shouted, "will you quit riding me? You've been preaching that all my life, and I'm sick of it. If you want to be a workaholic, fine, but I'm not going to sell my soul to any company!"

Any learning Brad might have done from his job loss was short-circuited.

If Brad's father had been a helicopter, he might have said, "Gee, Brad, that's terrible. Tell you what. I found that job for you and I can probably find another. I've got a friend I can check with. Meanwhile, how much money do you need to tide you over the next couple of weeks?"

LOVE AND LOGIC TIP 3
Consequences with Empathy

Children learn from their mistakes when:

❖ *They experience the consequences of their mistakes; and*
❖ *Adults in their environment provide empathy.*

Bad choices have natural consequences. If David fails to wear a coat, he gets cold. If Jan misses the school bus, she stays home, with an unexcused absence for the day.

Adults are tempted to scold and reprimand, but may be surprised to learn that children actually learn best from consequences when adults empathize:

❖ *"I'm so sorry you're cold, David."*
❖ *"What a bummer that you missed an after-school party on the day you were absent, Jan."*

If adults reprimand them, children may transform sorrow over their choice into anger with the adult—and the lesson may be lost. If adults express sorrow, children have a significant learning opportunity. David may think, "Tomorrow I'll wear my coat." Jan may decide, "I'll get up fifteen minutes earlier tomorrow."

Consequences + Empathy = Learning

Again, the process of Brad's learning from the consequences—perhaps that he needs to look at his work habits—would have been short-circuited since his father is always there to fix things for him.

If Brad's dad had been a consultant, he might have said, "Brad, that's terrible. It must be frightening to have a family and be without a guaranteed income. I'm so sorry. What are you going to do?"

With empathy from his father, Brad could have faced the realities of his frayed work ethic, suffered the consequences, and then, done some growing.

❦ *Limit #3*
Offer genuine sorrow and empathy.
This drives the pain of the consequence into the heart,
where it can be converted into wisdom.

Johnny Finds His Way

Johnny, who lived with his grandparents, came home from school with a failing report card. His grandfather, turning into a drill sergeant, said, "No kid in this family gets grades like this! You are grounded until you bring those grades up!"

Put yourself in Johnny's shoes. All Johnny could think of was Grandpa's reaction, instead of thinking about what he needed to focus on: His life, and how he was going to change his study habits.

Instead, Grandpa could approach this situation with empathy: "Boy, you must feel awful about those. Maybe it's embarrassing for you, and I'll bet it was hard for you to bring that report card home to me. Tell you what, though. You know I'll love you no matter how many years it takes you to get through sixth grade. Now give me a hug."

Johnny, knowing he is loved, immediately focuses on his life. "Years!" he says. "I don't have years to get through sixth grade. My friends will go on to seventh!"

"You don't need them—you've got me," Grandpa comforts him.

Secure in his grandfather's love, Johnny is now able to look at his life. He is determined to not be left behind. To prove it, he brings his books home to study, completes assignments on time, and goes on to seventh grade with the rest of his class.

Linear and Cyclical Consequences

TWO KINDS OF MISTAKES

There are two kinds of mistakes that happen between you and your adult children and grandchildren:

LOVE AND LOGIC TIP 4
Who Owns the Problem?

The list of problems children own is endless: Getting to school on time, getting to school at all, dropping out of school, hassling or being hassled by friends, harassing or being harassed by teachers, poor grades, laziness, wrong choice in friends—we could go on and on. The major combatants in conflict are either:

1. *the child and others, or*
2. *the child and him- or herself.*

Grandparents who involve themselves in these problems can expend a lot of excess energy. They believe that jumping into such conflicts and rescuing their grandkids demonstrates their love.

It's important to remember, however, that everything we fix for children, they are unable to fix for themselves. If there is more than a 10 percent chance that a child might be able to work out his or her own problem, we should stay clear of it.

The list of childhood problems that adults own is fairly short. It includes events that directly affect the adult—such as back-talk, failure to do assigned chores, messes in their environment, voice volume levels that cause discomfort, and damage to their property.

For problems that affect the adult directly, the adult must take action—to take care of his or her own needs. If a child's behavior is a problem for the adult, it should be a problem for the child as well. The adult can remove the child from hearing range in a time-out, ask for payment for damages, or expect chores to be completed—all in a tone of discipline rather than punishment.

❖ Those that cause a problem only for the child or grandchild who makes the mistake, and

❖ Those that also cause a problem for you.

It is essential to recognize which one has occurred in order to deal with the situation in an effective manner. If the situation causes a problem only for the child or grandchild, it is appropriate for you to stay out of it, encouraging the child to learn from his or her mistake. If the situation creates a problem for you, then it is appropriate for you to get involved.

Further, the way you handle each situation can determine whether the consequences will be *linear* or *cyclical*. A linear outcome means that particular bad choice probably will not be made again. If the outcome is cyclical, that bad choice is likely to repeat itself.

The following diagrams illustrate these differences.

When we act as a helicopter or drill sergeant, we actually encourage our loved ones to cyclically repeat their mistakes again and again. More concerned with the way we acted in the situation and how that made them feel, they are less able to focus on their real problem. When we act as consultants, we walk beside our loved ones in a straight line, supporting them with love and heart-felt attention, allowing them to suffer the consequences of a mistake and take appropriate action.

❦ *It is a wise grandparent who can allow a bad choice to belong to a grandchild or adult child, which gives that child the opportunity to learn how to deal with it.*

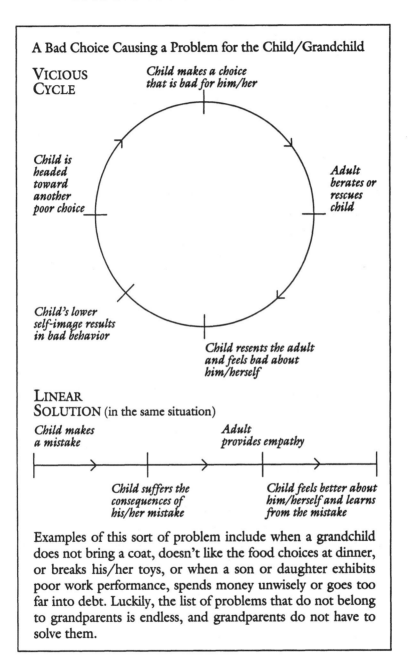

A Bad Choice Causing a Problem for the Child/Grandchild

VICIOUS CYCLE

Child makes a choice that is bad for him/her

Child is headed toward another poor choice

Adult berates or rescues child

Child's lower self-image results in bad behavior

Child resents the adult and feels bad about him/herself

LINEAR SOLUTION (in the same situation)

Child makes a mistake

Adult provides empathy

Child suffers the consequences of his/her mistake

Child feels better about him/herself and learns from the mistake

Examples of this sort of problem include when a grandchild does not bring a coat, doesn't like the food choices at dinner, or breaks his/her toys, or when a son or daughter exhibits poor work performance, spends money unwisely or goes too far into debt. Luckily, the list of problems that do not belong to grandparents is endless, and grandparents do not have to solve them.

When a Bad Choice of a Child/Grandchild Also Makes a Problem for You.

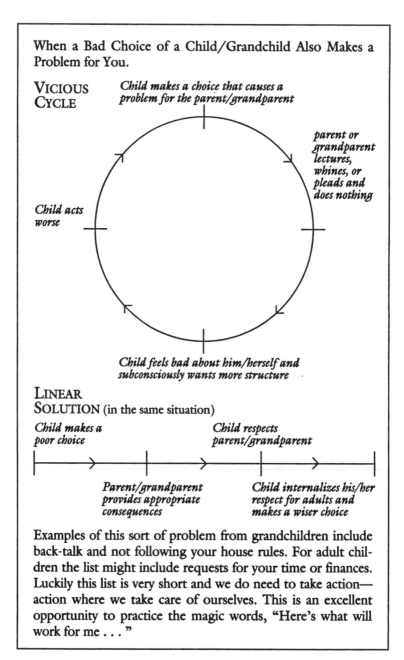

VICIOUS CYCLE

Child makes a choice that causes a problem for the parent/grandparent

parent or grandparent lectures, whines, or pleads and does nothing

Child acts worse

Child feels bad about him/herself and subconsciously wants more structure

LINEAR SOLUTION (in the same situation)

Child makes a poor choice

Child respects parent/grandparent

Parent/grandparent provides appropriate consequences

Child internalizes his/her respect for adults and makes a wiser choice

Examples of this sort of problem from grandchildren include back-talk and not following your house rules. For adult children the list might include requests for your time or finances. Luckily this list is very short and we do need to take action— action where we take care of ourselves. This is an excellent opportunity to practice the magic words, "Here's what will work for me . . ."

A Five-Step Rehearsal

At first, grandparenting with Love and Logic may seem like an overwhelming change. Instead of allowing your familial relationships to run on automatic pilot, you now have to think about enforceable limits, choices, techniques, and consequences with empathy.

Further, sometimes a child or grandchild may sense your shift and resent it. One son, when his father chose not to rescue him from financial debacle, said, "Dad, this isn't like you."

"I know, son," said his father. "But give me three months, and it *will* be!"

Trying to act on these principles all at once is enough to frustrate anyone. Love and Logic grandparenting is like dieting. Dieters do not say, "I am going to become thin today," and presto, become thin. Likewise, grandparents cannot promise, "I'm going to grandparent with Love and Logic 100 percent of the time."

If the principles of Love and Logic are new to you, we prescribe a small dose at a time. Pick one problem that bothers you about your child or grandchild. Focus on it and work on it. Here is a five-step rehearsal plan to help you.

A FIVE-STEP REHEARSAL PLAN

1. Pick a situation that causes you stress.
2. Choose one from the following Love and Logic techniques:

❖ Enforceable limits
❖ Choices
❖ Consequences with empathy

3. Imagine the sound of your voice.
4. Try it out on friends and get their responses.
5. Rehearse until you feel ready.

If you're not sure what your rehearsal should sound like or exactly what you would say, relax. In the chapters that follow, you will find many sample Love and Logic responses to a number of situations.

Underlying all of Love and Logic are two essential messages:

The Primary Message:
"I love you, and I hope your life goes well."

The Secondary Message:
"You are the kind of person who can learn from your mistakes. You are bright enough to learn and strong enough to handle the pain that comes from unwise choices you've made."

In the long term, Love and Logic grandparenting is a source of empowerment for our loved ones as well as ourselves. Practicing its principles helps us take better care of ourselves and those around us, clarify problem areas, and improve our relationships with one another. In today's world, we need as much of this as we can get. And what better place to start than at home, with the people who mean the most to us.

⮞2⮜

Raising Kids
Today

Train up a child in the way he should go;
and when he is old he will not depart from it.
—Proverbs, XXII, 6

When I (Jim) became a parent, for a few years I walked around shaking my head, saying, "I can't understand it. It worked for my dad. Why doesn't it work for me?"

When my dad said, "Jump!" I asked, "How high?" and "How many times?" I followed orders. That worked for him, and I will never fault him for the way he raised me. He did the best he could, and his style was appropriate for the times.

The times, however, have changed. Is raising kids today like it was a generation ago? No way! It's a different world out there, and the changes in our society have altered our kids, which has forced us to alter our parenting. To be effective grandparents, we need to be aware of what it means to be a parent and a child these days.

Parents' Concerns and Children's Rights

Because the parenting environment has radically deviated from what it used to be, parents have lost confidence. They have become uncertain—unsure of themselves and their decisions. They are worried about doing irreparable damage to their children as they raise them, and about violating the law when disciplining them.

🍎 *In the past decade, our society's emphasis has switched from a parent-centered to a child-centered environment.*

Raising a child with a positive self-concept has become of paramount concern. Parents are hesitant to say no for fear of damaging their child's self-concept.

Jeannie's Fit

A parent raising a three-year-old recently said to me (Jim), "I can't get Jeannie to go to her room."

I told her, "Tell her she has a choice of how to go to her room—with her feet touching the floor or with her feet not touching the floor."

That mother looked at me with big eyes and said, "But she'll be upset and throw a fit!"

I said, "You bet she'll throw a fit! If she's worth keeping, she'll throw a fit."

This mom said, "But she'll be so unhappy. What about her self-concept?"

Having a positive self-concept does not mean your child is never going to be unhappy. Life has many unhappy moments and you want your children to know how to deal with them when they happen. A child experienced in life's unending choice-making and decision-making is more likely to have a strong self-concept than one with none.

Adding weight to parental fear is a new set of legal rulings in favor of children's rights. Parents now are not only afraid of damaging their children's self-concepts, but of breaking the law. The human rights issue can tie parental hands.

I Have Rights

One parent became impatient when he wanted to sleep and his teenage son was blaring the stereo at 2:00 a.m. When he suggested that his son turn the music down, his son said, "I don't have to. This is my home too. I have rights."

This father could have said, "Nice try, but if if you really believe you own this home, check the name on the mortgage. Do you want to turn that music down, or do you want to turn it off?" This parent did nothing because he had heard about children's rights, about children suing parents for divorce, and he was afraid to act.

Our concerns about self-concept and children's rights have caused the pendulum to swing off center. When I (Jim), as a young boy, told my dad, "I don't have to do that, I have rights," he answered, "No, you don't. Wait until you grow up. Then you'll have rights."

When I went to school and asked my classmates what *their* parents said, I was told they said the same thing. When I asked my teachers, they confirmed my dad's view. So, I thought, "Must be right." That was the end of that.

Today, when an adolescent checks out that attitude, it will be contradicted. His peers will say, "No way, man! You don't have to take that!" And the school counselor will tell him he has rights. The counselor will even tell him what they are.

In the past, if a 16-year-old threatened his parents, they could tell the teenager to leave home. Today, that is against the law. It is also against the law to require a child to sleep overnight in a tent, in the garage, or on the porch. If a child chooses to do so, then it's all right. In some cases, spanking or causing a child to miss a meal could be considered child abuse.

Children today are aware that they have these rights. And they know at a young age. A six-year-old, roughhousing with my granddaughter and me (Foster) one day, said to me in jest, "You'd better watch out, or I'll report you for child abuse." At six, she knew her power.

Solving the Confidence Crisis

In the past, the maxim was, "Children should be seen and not heard." The unspoken maxim of today is, "Children have a right to be heard, whenever they wish, and at whatever volume they wish."

For parents, this child-centered family model and the children's rights movement produce a confidence crisis. This lethal and paralyzing combination leaves parents confused about how to effectively discipline their children.

Is a child's self-concept important? Yes. But self-concept is not something you install in a child like software on a computer hard drive. It comes from gradually handling responsibilities well, making decisions and living with them, doing chores and getting through struggles.

🍎 *Adults don't contribute to a child's bad self-concept by saying "no". The bad self-concept comes when adults provide no consequences for their child's poor choices.*

When kids say, "I've got rights," mothers and fathers can assure them of those rights—but on parents' terms—setting enforceable limits and offering choices that are

---

LOVE AND LOGIC TIP 5
Better Ways to Say "No"

The word "no" triggers resistance more easily than any other word in the English language. It's a child's call to arms. Children hear it far too often—so often that it's the first word many kids learn to say.

When they hear "no," half the time they ignore it. Having heard it so much, they come to think it means "maybe." Other times they think it really means "yes."

A good rule for "no" is to use it as seldom as possible. When you do use it, make sure you mean business. All the other times, you can make a statement positively and still deny a request. You are saying "yes" instead of "no," but you are still in control. The behavior you want can be established without triggering resistance. Here are two examples:

No Statement: *"No, you may not go out to play until you practice your lessons."*
Yes Statement: *"Yes, you may go out to play as soon as you practice your lessons."*

❖ ❖ ❖

No Statement: *"No, you may not watch television until the dishes are done."*
Yes Statement: *"Yes, you may watch television as soon as the dishes are done."*

What a difference a turn of the phrase can make in how a child learns and responds!

---

within the range of acceptable behavior. Then, the confidence crisis is solved for both children and adults.

Love and Logic parenting and grandparenting can help parents raise children in today's world by bringing the pendulum closer to the center. Children have a right to be heard, and at a volume that does not destroy anyone's eardrums. Parents have a right to be heard and to set house rules. After all, if God had meant children to run the family, they would have been born bigger.

Society Has Changed

Part of the reason parenting is different in today's world is that parents have less disposable time than a generation ago. The average parent has 50 hours less free time per month than a decade ago. People who are working have less free time too. When both parents are working, often there is no parent home with a child. During school years, many children of working parents become "latchkey" kids, letting themselves in and baby-sitting themselves after school, until a parent comes home.

Parents have less unscheduled time; yet, society sets a high priority on spending time with children. The result: parental guilt.

🍎 *Today's parents carry around more guilt
about the way they parent than their parents did.*

You can guess that this results in an even greater loss of confidence and stronger feelings of uncertainty.

THE ONLY WORLD THEY KNOW

Consider that this is the only world our grandchildren know—a world far different from the one we grew up in—a world of constant, accelerating change. As a result, messages about morals and authority are in constant flux. In the 1950s, we lived in a "Pinocchio" society. When Pinocchio told lies, his nose got bigger. Other people could immediately see he was lying. When he became brave and honest, he achieved his goal—to become a real boy.

Later came the "Life of Riley" society, which proclaimed that fathers were foolish and kids were wise. Today, this message has evolved to the point that kids are not only the smartest in the family, they are *the* ones to be listened to and reckoned with. Children now believe that they don't have to listen to adults and that goals are reached through manipulation.

Technology has altered the way we see things. There is a communication explosion. Television, videos, video games and computers are all part of the new Information Age. Kids live in the fast-paced world of electronic stimulation. Video cassettes—kids' interaction of choice—have become baby-sitters. There isn't a study that doesn't show that kids spend more time with TV than in school, or with their parents.

Our environment today is more competitive than ever before. Professional sports loom large. Players are role models—heroes. Who won last night's game, or which players get paid the most, is more important than world events. Sports competitions are offered to kids at a younger and younger age, as are competitions to be the prettiest and wear the latest expensive athletic shoes, or be the most popular in a group. The eyes of the country are focused on clothes and cosmetic models—"the beautiful people"—or on the music group that has the hottest video.

Sadly, children also live in a world with lower academic standards than ever before. ACT (college entrance exam) scores continue to drop, and universities are saying that many incoming freshmen need to spend their first year in remedial classes.

PRESSURES OF THE YOUTH CULTURE
Children face new pressures. Here are some samples.

Gangs: Many kids feel a tremendous pressure to join a gang. In the absence of close family interaction, gangs provide a support system that may be seen as a way the youngster can feel safe in a violent school or neighborhood.

Guns: This is the first time in United States history that kids have had a reason to feel unsafe on a daily basis. Hundreds of schools have metal detectors. In the past, kids might have settled a problem with their fists. Today they use guns.

Sex: Sex has lost its aura of mystery. By age 13, one-fifth of teens are no longer virgins. Studies show that 50 percent of all teen girls are sexually active, as are 65 percent of the boys.

Drugs & Alcohol: An enormous social problem, drugs and alcohol are easily available to young people everywhere. In 1993 alone, in the United States, 450,000 teens were cited for drunk driving.

Suicide: The leading cause of death among teens is suicide. Teens who commit suicide are most often those who have high expectations for themselves and don't measure up to them. Their real selves do not match their ideal selves.

🌶 *One important way parents and grandparents can help lessen the chance of a child's or grandchild's suicide is to communicate to them, "I love you and I accept you even though I cannot accept your behavior."*

But you can't just say it. You have to live it.

With all this peer pressure, are kids truly worse today? In a word, yes. When a 15-year-old takes a gun to school and uses it to settle a dispute, it doesn't take an expert to see that this does not bode well.

The good news is, while the bad are worse, the good kids are better. They have access to more information. They run faster, jump higher and know more. More magazines cater to them, and they have CD Roms to learn from. They understand more about the complexities of human relationships and are more responsive and caring.

Today we have a wider divergence of kids. As grandparents, one of our goals can be to help our grandchildren continue to grow on the better end of the spectrum.

Three Basic Needs Remain the Same

Despite change, there are basic needs that remain constant in our children. Are they still fighting with their siblings? Do they still want attention? Do they continue to want to hear stories that provide them with a sense of identity? Yes. Yes. Yes. Kids still experience universal feelings of anxiety, pride, prejudice, embarrassment, greed, love, ungratefulness and commitment. Their world still has rituals of passage for birth, puberty, marriage, and death. All children continue to have three basic needs: for control, inclusion and affection.

Control. A car salesman knows about giving control. From the moment you step on the lot, you are asked questions that put you in the driver's seat: "What kind of car do you have in mind?" he asks you. Then he offers control in bite-size pieces. "A two-door or a four-door?" "What color?" "Manual transmission or automatic?" "What price range?" With each question he gives you more control. All these questions have helped you meet your control needs. Eventually you buy the control rather than the car.

It is this same control that children look for. When they don't have healthy control through choices, within limits, they become insecure. They tire of being told what to do and how to do it, without being asked for their opinions. Never in a position of control, they hunger for and search out their first chance—any chance—to jump into the driver's seat, sometimes taking the wheel when they don't know how to drive.

Inclusion. Inclusion is a basic human need that makes gangs attractive. Every child needs a group to identify with, a place he or she belongs, or a situation that fits. When children do not find this sense of inclusion in the home, they look for it on the streets, or with peer groups— some of which are bad influences. We adults are no different. We have needs for inclusion, too. We fill ours by finding churches, clubs, bowling leagues, or drinking buddies.

LOVE AND LOGIC TIP 6
The "V" of Love and Control

In the "V" of love, the limits we set for our children diminish as the years go by. By the time they become adults, they should be completely free of our control. Unfortunately, when we see our adult children making unwise choices, some of us are tempted to retrieve a bit of control to straighten things out. The result, however, is unhappy adult children and strained relations.

Understanding the "V" of love and control also helps in relating to our grandchildren, as they learn, every day, a little at a time, how to take charge of their own lives.

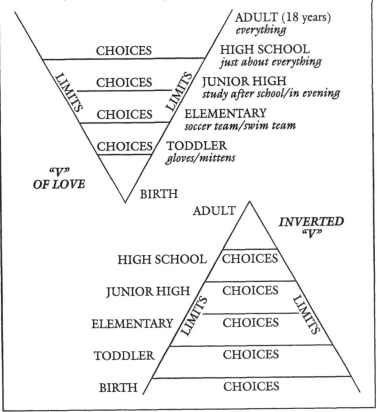

We all want attention and long to be recognized for who we are. And why shouldn't we have that?

Affection. Children of all ages are in desperate need of smiles and hugs. They know whether or not they are loved and appreciated, because they have an extra sensory perception of this feeling that goes beyond verbal communication.

GRANDPARENTS CAN HELP FILL THESE NEEDS

Grandparents are especially suited to meeting the three basic needs of children. Most not only have more time to spend but have the benefit of their past experiences in raising their own children. Love and Logic grandparents can offer their grandkids:

1. *Control*—by giving choices and setting enforceable limits, which teach children decision-making and compromise.

2. *Inclusion*—by working on projects with grandchildren. Whether sweeping the floor or working on a car engine, when children are involved in an adult project, they feel included. It's as simple as that.

3. *Affection*—by taking the time and energy to provide the hugs, the smiles, the eye contact, and communication that a child hungers for.

As a consultant grandparent, you have the opportunity to fill an essential part of the basic needs your grandchildren may be missing, living in our time, our society, our world. Your attention to the basics they need can help them grow into better, stronger, and wiser members of the new generation. We think that's a goal worth the effort.

Grandparenting Today

The trees in the streets are old trees used to living with people,
Family trees that remember your grandfather's name.
—Stephen Vincent Benét
"John Brown's Body"

Today, we grandparents tend to move toward the twenty-first century with images of "Grandparenting Past": Silver-haired, slow-talking, slow-moving people biding their time in wooden rocking chairs on the front porch, contemplating the sunset through wire-rimmed spectacles. They smile crinkly smiles and take out their teeth at night. Grandmothers crochet booties and make cookies, while grandfathers whittle wooden treasures with jackknives. Their grandchildren walk over from across town, sit on the porch with them, admire the carving and munch on the cookies.

Grandparents: More Important Than Ever

Each of us carries variations of this picture created in our own childhood. As we set the zoom feature on our cameras to "Grandparenting Present," we realize with shock how much the picture has changed. We travel around the world instead of crochet, or play golf instead of whittle. Some of us become grandparents long before we are ready for rocking chairs. Many of our grandchildren live half a continent away, or wear strange baggy clothes in radical color combinations and pierce their ears.

Consider these statistics:

❖ Ninety-four percent of older adults with children in the United States have grandchildren. Half of these are great-grandparents.[4]

❖ Of the 54 million grandparents in the United States, 26 percent are younger than age 55. Only 38 percent are in their retirement years (over 65).[5]

❖ The average grandparent has three or four grandchildren.[6]

❖ Grandparents are living longer; from 1940 to 1980 the life expectancy for a 40-year-old woman increased by seven years, and life expectancy for a 40-year-old man by four years.

What do these numbers mean? Grandparents are more important than ever. More adults than ever are living long enough to get to know their grandchildren, and for their grandchildren to get to know them. This increase in longevity is giving their relationships the potential to become stronger and longer lasting.

These relationships are growing more important not only to grandparents, but to grandchildren as well. Recent studies reveal a finding you will want to know:

🍎 *Children close to at least one grandparent are more emotionally secure than those without such a tie.*[7]

Today's grandparenting has changed because we have changed, and because our grandchildren and their world have changed. In this new world, the roles grandparents play can vary widely. Some have grandkids just down the street who stop in regularly on their way home from school. Others see them two to three times a year, during family trips and holidays. Still others have adult children and grandchildren living with them, making them parents a second time around. Other grandparents live in blended families with biological grandchildren and step-grandchildren, which include other sets of grandparents. Whatever your situation, in a world of rapid change, your grandchildren need you more than ever before.

David Elkind has observed that there are three kinds of societies:[8] those with little change, moderate change, and rapid change. In fixed societies with little change, grandparents are considered wise guides, people who pass on wisdom from the past.

In societies with moderate change, children look to grandparents and parents for wisdom, but also rely on their peers. In societies with rapid change, the young, who spend most of their time adapting to what is new, often lose respect for older generations and become alienated from them.

In rapidly changing societies, it is the young who lose, says Elkind. This doesn't have to be true in your family. You can help by remembering the following:

Grandparents can provide stability by:

◆ Listening—truly listening—to their grandchildren.
◆ Refusing to compete in the acquisition of material possessions.
◆ Giving their most valuable gift—time.

Grandparent Roles and Lifestyles

A look at roles and styles of grandparenting will help give each of us a sense of where we fit in the wide range of grandparenting behavior. Berniece Neugarten and Karol Wesinstein have identified the following six roles grandparents most often play:[9]

FORMAL

Formal grandparents follow what they regard as proper and prescribed behavior for grandparents. Occasionally they provide special treats, or a minor service such as baby-sitting. They keep clear lines, however, between parenting and grandparenting. They leave parenting strictly to the parent. Although they are interested in the grandchild, they are careful to not to offer advice on child rearing.

FUN-SEEKER

Fun-seekers approach grandparenting with a spirit of informality and playfulness. They see grandchildren as a source of leisure activity and become adult play-mates. Authority lines are irrelevant; their primary interest is in the mutual satisfaction of their relationship with their grandchildren. One grandmother put it this way. "I leave for the parents the peanut butter and jelly of daily life. It's my turn, at last, to be a chocolate." Another said, "It's my second chance at parenting—my chance this time to love, without conditions, without strings attached."[10]

RESERVOIR OF FAMILY WISDOM

In more authoritarian family structures, a grandparent can become a resource for teaching skills or passing on family traditions. This grandparent plays the role of wise counselor—the clan leader.

DISTANT FIGURE

Some grandparents emerge from the shadows only on holidays and other special occasions. For many families, grandparents' presence brings comfort and lends a sense of ritual stability to the extended family. Grandmoms and dads are markers on the horizon.

FAMILY PILLAR

A move, or family crisis, their health, age of their grandchildren, financial status, or status of their adult children—any or all of these can affect the part a grand-parent plays and change it in a second. During times of crisis, grandparents may take on a more active role, becoming family pillars, sources of strength and stability. In a divorce, maternal grandparents often become a source of child care as well as financial and emotional support for mother and child.

SURROGATE PARENT

In such extreme situations, some grandparents—and primarily grandmothers—play the part of substitute parent. Perhaps a mother goes to work, and the grandparent provides day care. Or, due to parental incapacity, a grandparent may become custodian of a grandchild on a temporary or permanent basis.

In one study of grandparenting styles, a researcher discovered that half of all grandparents chose either the fun-seeker or the distant figure role.[11] The reason? Many parents have a strong reluctance to share the raising of their children with extended family and neighbors. Yet, ironically, many of these same parents readily dump parental responsibilities onto schools and other government institutions. The sad result is that these parents not only do not have the support they need, but extended family and community are fearful of involving themselves with children other than their own. Who are the losers in these situations? The children, of course. Their basic needs are not met by parents, grandparents, school, or community.

Another discovery is that when families stayed in their neighborhood over longer periods of time, the whole community, including neighbors and grandparents, tended to take more responsibility for the children's development.

Now, with more single parents than ever, and more homes with both parents working, there is a great deal of re-thinking going on with regard to the importance of the grandparent role. Parents, in particular, play a crucial role in the quality of the grandchild-grandparent relationship. If grandparents' relationships with their children are intact, the children are more likely to allow their own children and their parents to enjoy time with one another. If a grandparent's relationship with his or her adult child is severed or strained, there is less likelihood of relating well with grandchildren.

Sources of Grandparent Satisfaction

Grandparents who play these different roles often find benefits and sources of enjoyment they never imagined could come from visiting with their grandchildren. If you are a grandparent, you may have already made these discoveries on your own.

BIOLOGICAL RENEWAL[12]

Just by spending time with their grandchildren, many grandparents feel biologically renewed. They are inspired to be playful, involved, good listeners and active participants. Mental stimulation seems to lead to physical renewal.

EMOTIONAL FULFILLMENT

Others feel emotional fulfillment, perhaps because their bond with a grandchild meets their need for interacting with other people. Many researchers have observed that a grandchild's success or failure in the larger world is not as crucial to the grandparent as the child's involvement with him or her in this special one-to-one relationship.

TEACHER OR RESOURCE PERSON

Many grandparents find significance in being a teacher, a resource person, sharing their skills and knowledge, boosting their own self-concept. Whether a grandparent has been a farmer, a homemaker, a lawyer, a fire fighter, a salesperson, a butcher, baker, or candlestick maker—each has something to teach. No matter what their occupation or job, each has been a parent and a child, and has a wealth of information about life.

VICARIOUS ACHIEVEMENT

A number of grandparents find satisfaction from no more than basking in the glow of reflected glory when their grandchildren do well on a test, earn honorable mention, win a difficult battle, or demonstrate intelligence, wit, or humor. The fact that they share similar genes is reward enough.

The Grandparent Paradox

The bond between child and grandparent can indeed be the purest, least complicated form of human love. But that bond is part of a more complicated web of family relationships and lifestyles. As a result, two-thirds of grandparents express great satisfaction with their roles, yet one-third have sufficient dissatisfaction to mention it in surveys.

While grandparents value family ties and kinship, they also value their independence and autonomy. Sometimes the two values clash. They are asked to baby-sit on the very Saturday afternoon they planned to play golf. They've just begun to enjoy the peace of an empty nest when a divorced daughter wants to move back home with her two children. Their needs are in direct conflict with those of their adult children and grandchildren, and they feel torn. That double bind may come from their adult children as well.

In a study asking parents about the best and worst aspects of grandparent roles in their family, here's what they offered.[12]

Best Things About Grandparents

❖ Provide help and support when needed
❖ Strengthen the family
❖ Relate well with grandchildren
❖ Share their experience, creating a sense of
   family heritage

Worst Things About Grandparents

❖ Interfere and advise
❖ Create conflict with grandchildren
❖ Provide a feeling of distance within the family

This study points to an interesting paradox for grandparents. While adult children's most appreciation was for grandparents' help and support, their greatest problem was with their interference. The line between support and interference can be a thin one. What is intended as support can be interpreted as butting in. How does a grandparent find a balance?

It is in resolving this double bind that a Love and Logic approach to grandparenting can be crucial.

The Consultant Grandparent:
- ❖ Works with enforceable limits, choices, and consequences—all with empathy.
- ❖ Decides to balance need for autonomy and kinship.
- ❖ Finds her or his limits and then tells adult children what those limits are.
- ❖ Understands the difference between support and interference.

The Helicopter or Drill Sergeant Grandparent:
- ❖ Criticizes adult children in front of their own children.
- ❖ Provides unsolicited advice.
- ❖ Undermines parental house rules.
- ❖ Lowers behavioral standards of the children.

We often find that when people find a friend with whom they can discuss differences, they learn new approaches. The next time you are with a friend you think might have some good ideas, strike up a conversation. Here are some positive and negative actions to fuel the fire of your discussion.

Positive	*Negative*
Offer empathy	Criticize
Give support	Interfere
Listen	Give unsolicited advice
Consultant	Drill sergeant/Helicopter

At this point, you may be wondering whether you can honestly determine the difference between support and interference, and you may be questioning whether you have been offering support that has been interpreted as interference.

As you read on, we believe you will come to clearly see the difference and learn how to tell the two apart. In Chapter 4, we will go over ways to bond with your grandchild that are supportive rather than interfering. And in Chapter 5, we will get into even more detail about appropriate times for grandparents to act.

≈4≈

Bonding With Today's Grandchild

T.T.T.
Put up in a place
Where it's easy to see
The cryptic admonishment
T. T. T.
When you feel how depressingly
Slowly you climb,
It's well to remember that
Things Take Time.[13]
—Piet Hein
from *Grooks*

Our fast-paced world seems to beg for a way to bond at super-glue speed. Relationships, however, are not built that quickly. Bonding, like all good things, takes time. Little by little, adding a bit here and a chunk there, time spent together grows like those silver balls we used to make with chewing gum wrapping paper.

Building A Bond

If we live close to our grandchildren, those bits of time may be frequent and short. If we live far away, we may get small chunks followed by long separations.

No matter what size your chunks of time with your grandchildren, bonding requires an ingredient few adults provide for children: attention. Kids are on the periphery of many events in our world. Because pre-adolescent children think in concrete, literary ways, many adult conversations can go over their heads. Sermon discussions, political small talk, and descriptions of professional sports may float far above their understanding.

❧ *Often, children are present, but not participating.*

In focusing on our grandchildren, we invest ourselves in them and in their futures. Since we are living in a world of busier and busier parents, the time children spend with their grandparents becomes more and more valuable. Grandparents can center on a child, get down on one knee, look him or her in the eye, ask questions and listen to the answers—all of which are part of giving one of the most important gifts of all: focused attention.

Mutual projects. The manner of bonding is different for every set of grandparent and child. For some, projects they do together work well. They bake cookies, clean the kitchen, and enjoy the leftover batter on the cookie spoon. Together they build a wooden car, sand it, paint it, and test its speed on the sidewalk in front of Grandpa's house.

There is great likelihood that you are the last generation in your family to have grown up without television. Grandchildren may be amazed to discover that was possible. You can pass on the things you did instead. Kids are intrigued that grandparents are extraordinary people who know how to build houses out of tongue depressors and make play stores out of empty cereal cartons and aluminum cans. They also know how to make toy telephones out of those cans.

Grandparents can offer their grandkids skills that only they have. One grandfather we know spends a couple of hours a week teaching his grandson woodworking. A teenager we know spent a week one summer building a radio-control airplane in his grandpa's basement. The teenager's grandmother said she was an "airplane widow" for the week they were holed up in the basement workshop, dusk to dawn. The special bond they built is far stronger and will undoubtedly last longer than the airplane.

For others, bonding takes place, not by making things, but through games and playing with toys, such as Pictionary, checkers, Scrabble, card games, or one-on-one basketball. Together they stack blocks and do puzzles.

Trips Together. Many grandchildren hold in their memories the special treasure of a trip alone with Grandpa and Grandma when they were between ages six and ten. That children's age-span seems to be the one at which such an outing is most likely to be enjoyed by both generations. Grandchildren benefit because they get to be around adults who are, most often, less harried, less rushed, less intense and more mellow than their parents.

At their frenetic, electronically stimulated age, that mellowness can provide them with a different model—inspire different thoughts, bring on different feelings.

Watch out though! Just as there is a thin line between support and interference, there is also a thin line between mellowness and boredom.

The Importance of Conversation

While you work, play and travel, you and your grandchildren can talk, interact with each other, and cement the bond that joins you. In these conversations, you will want to be aware of how well you follow three essential principles of effective communication.

Listen. Communication is more than sending words. It is also receiving them. When building a bond, receiving may be more important than sending. Our body language is an important factor in our listening. In fact, we listen with more than our ears; we listen with our eyes, our faces, and our whole bodies.
Example: Your grandchild is telling you how she ran in the 100-yard dash—and won. You are leaning forward, eyes on her face as she describes her win. Your eyes are opened wide, your jaw drops in amazement as she describes her sprint ahead, and your hands jump up to the sky in excitement as she tells you she *won!* Without uttering a word, you send a message of interest.

Understand. Work as hard as you can to do more than just hear your grandchild's words, but to understand what the child means and the importance of these words to him or her.

Example: Your grandchild John says, "I hate school." Instead of saying, "Oh, I used to hate school, too," patting him on the head and dismissing the whole thing, you might ask: "Why?" Does he mean he has a hard time socially? Academically? Is he frightened of a new situation? A person?

Prove you understand. Feedback is worth more than gold. If your grandkids hear their thoughts and feelings coming back in your words, they will know you understand, and that understanding will provide a connection they will never forget.

Example: "Jennie, that race was a real landmark for you. You practiced hard and reached your goal, didn't you!" Or, "John, sounds as if you have a good reason not to like school. What's going on? Somebody there troubling you?"

Brainstorming Consequences. If the issue a grandchild is discussing is a problem that needs solving, a fourth communication step may be helpful. You can help brainstorm the consequences of choices a grandchild is considering.

Jennie's Choice

When Jennie was feeling left out of the fourth-grade social scene at her school, her grandma said, "That's sad, Jennie. What do you think you're going to do?"

Jennie answered, "I don't know, Grandma."

Grandma then asked, "Would you like to hear what some other kids have tried when they've had that problem?"

Jennie nodded. Being the wise woman she is, Grandma knew it was best to offer some bad solutions before offering good ones.

"Some girls tell the teacher to force the students to let her play with them. How do you think that would work?"

Jennie shook her head. "That would just make them really nasty to me when the teacher isn't looking," she said.

They explored other possibilities—being nasty back to them, telling their parents, telling the other students how she felt, finding other friends. Jennie made the decision to cultivate a friendship with one girl, Karen, instead of trying to break into the clique.

HEART-TO-HEARTS

Not all interactions with grandchildren need to be lengthy. In fact, heart-to-heart talks that can eventually change a child's life and choices tend to be just the opposite. Most are short, sweet, and end with a question. Here's an example.

Jason and Aaron

Jason and his younger brother Aaron are visiting Grandpa for the morning and are locked into a teasing-fighting ritual. When Grandpa has Jason alone for a moment, he asks, "Do you ever worry that when Aaron grows up, he might hate your guts because the things you say make him fighting mad?" Then Grandpa gives him a little hug and sends him off to the swing to play.

Later Grandpa catches Aaron alone and asks him, "Do you ever worry that if you keep teasing Jason and taking his things without permission, which makes him really mad, that some day you could get hurt pretty bad?" Then he gives Aaron a little kiss and lets him head for the store with Grandma.

These short, sweet heart-to-hearts that end with a question encourage kids to think through issues for themselves. Aaron and Jason's choices about their behaviors are ultimately their own to make. By asking them brief questions that don't require on-the-spot responses, we help them think and act for themselves.

Pointing Up the Positives

When a grandparent criticizes a grandchild's parent in front of that child, the strongest grandparent-grandchild bond can dissolve in a minute. Children resent such criticism although they may not voice that resentment to you. Why? Because deep within they suspect that they will be the next subject for your critical remarks. "If she criticizes Dad, I'm sure she criticizes me when I'm not here."

When you find fault with your grandchild's parents you also take the risk that the child will see this as an opportunity to divide and conquer—perhaps use this information to fight the adult world and its authority.

Studies have shown that a warm relationship with your daughter or son enhances your bond with your grandchildren. Conversely, a strong bond with your grandchildren can enhance your relationship with your adult children. A woman, whose relationship with her parents had been tenuous and shaky, commented, when her children were young, "I can forgive my parents almost anything when I see how wonderful they are with my children."

❦ *When grandparents criticize a child's parents, all three generations lose. Build up the bond, and all three generations win.*

Sharing Family History

A final source of bonding for grandparents and grandchildren is the sense of social and family history they can share. One grandchild was fascinated to hear how her grandfather's grade-school class was dismissed so they could all gather outside to watch a Model-T "putt-putting" up the gravel road to the one-room school. It was the equivalent of her parent's class being interrupted to watch John Glenn's spacecraft land in the ocean following the world's first orbit.

A grandson enjoyed hearing stories about his grandfather's experiences aboard a submarine during World War II. Another grandchild enjoyed hearing stories about her parents when they were children—especially their daring escapades.

Whatever the stories, as long as they are a source of joy for both generations, you can keep telling them. You draw energy from the glow on their faces. As a result, the years peel away and, for a moment, you recapture your youth.

When grandchildren start to yawn, however, because they've heard this story many times or because they simply aren't interested, it's time for a quick change of pace. You want to keep a balance between what you tell them and what they tell you.

❦ *As you can pass on to your grandkids a sense of the past, they can give you a sense of the future.*

Applying The Three Basic Principles to Your Growing Grandchild

Preschoolers see their grandparents differently than adolescents do. Let's take a few moments to notice what these differences are.

Infancy (Birth to 18 Months). Newborns come into the world with reflexes and senses. Their reflexes include sucking, grasping, and startling at loud noises. They can recognize their mother's voice already at birth, and their senses of taste and touch are quite well developed. They use all their senses to explore their new world.

Nearsighted at this early age, infants' clearest vision is of objects 7 to 15 inches from their faces. In their first month, they rarely fix their gaze on the features of a person's face, but look around the periphery, such as the hairline. After their first month, they begin to focus on eyes and mouth.

Newborns don't automatically love parents, or grandparents, from birth. In the first 2 to 3 months, an infant may react the same to all adults, later learning to distinguish the primary caretaker, usually Mom. Somewhere between 5 and 12 months, many infants develop a fear of parting with Mom or a fear of strangers. Grandma and Grandpa, much to their chagrin, are sometimes part of that "stranger" group. Know that this is just a stage that soon will pass. Later, when you tell them they were once afraid of you, they'll laugh and refuse to believe it.

Infants enjoy sounds and rhythms of language long before they learn to talk, and nonsense rhymes are a source of real pleasure. So is peek-a-boo, especially because infants have no understanding of object permanence. When an object is out of sight, it ceases to exist, and they experience real surprise and shock when what ceased to exist suddenly recreates itself.

At about three months, they learn to roll over; at six months, they sit; and at around a year, they begin to walk.

In their second year, they gain a sense of object permanence and hunt for hidden objects. They begin speaking in words, using whole words to mean sentences, and they can respond to simple requests.

Infancy is a time of joy in new life, a new generation to continue the family line and traits. In this time of nursery rhymes and peek-a-boos, a foundation is laid for the time when grandchildren will begin to recognize their grandparents as special people.

Toddler and Preschool Years *(18 Months to 5 Years).* In these years children learn motor skills. As their large muscle skills increase, they learn to jump, skip, ride a tricycle, even a bicycle. Growth in small muscle skills allows them to fill sand pails, build with blocks, eat with a fork and spoon, dress themselves, and tie their shoelaces.

They also learn concepts and categories. Chairs are different from tables. A plate of four cookies is better than a plate of two cookies. They learn to follow simple instructions, such as, "Go to your room, and you will see the Teddy bear in the corner." They begin to see cause and effect: touching a hot pan makes for burned fingers.

In a preschooler's world, everything has a purpose. And it is either all good or all bad. Objects have life. Two events at the same time are assumed to be related:

if they clapped their hands and the phone rang, they believe they must have caused it to ring.

Toddlers learn language. They put words together to form sentences. They may not use all correct sounds, so grandparents sometimes need parents to serve as translators. These tiny tots may also make up their own terms for certain things. A blanket may be a furry sheet; an airplane may be a choo-choo bird.

Although these children may not understand the biological relationship between themselves and their grandparents, they come to see Grandpa and Grandma as special people in their lives. Toddler memories are fairly short; therefore, many grandparents try to keep their image frequently present for toddler grandchildren. If Grandma and Grandpa can't be there in person, they send a picture for the refrigerator, or make a telephone call.

LOVE AND LOGIC TIP 7
Affordable Price Tags

It's important for children to learn to make wise choices while they are young, when their mistakes have smaller price tags. If an adult loans a grade-school child money for rollerblades, the adult can create a real loan situation like "First National Bank"—drawing up a promissory note with a payment due date and a repossession clause.

If the child misses the payment due date, the adult becomes the owner of a pair of rollerblades, and the child learns a lesson in financial responsibility—while the price is still affordable. Learning that lesson with a $100 set of wheels at age 10 may save that child from having to learn that lesson over a $15,000 set of wheels later on.

Childhood (5 to 11 years). Erik Ericson sees childhood as the "industry" years. In his analysis of personality development, toddlerhood is the time for developing autonomy, preschool years for initiative, and childhood for developing an interest in doing practical and constructive things, such as cooking, fishing, sewing, and constructing models.

During these years, children learn to play games with rules. These are the years during which psychologists describe children's thinking as "concrete operations" because they take everything literally. Children at this age do not think abstractly about the nature of justice, but they certainly let it be known when they think they've been treated unfairly.

Around ages 8 to 9, children's peer groups begin to become more important to them, and their ability to solve problems grows. These are golden years for grandparents, because they are fully recognized as special people. These are the years of joint projects and outings. It is often during these years that granddaughters form a special bond with their grandmothers, as do grandsons with their grandfathers.

Adolescence (11 to 18). In adolescence, the peer group becomes the authoritative group. Grandchildren become critical of their parents and grandparents. As they experience rapid intellectual and physical growth, their thinking moves from concrete operations to "formal operations." They can understand literary images and think in abstractions. They construct abstract ideals—ideals to which previous generations fail to measure up.

This is a time when adolescents construct a personal

identity and believe that their social universe revolves around only them. They become preoccupied with the way others view them. A spot on their jeans at a party can be a source of total mortification. Their sense of identity may include a personal fable that causes them to believe they are unique or invulnerable. Many a great American novel has been attempted by an adolescent under the influence of such a fable.

These can be difficult years for grandparents as well as parents. As peer groups become more important to their grandkids, adults may see less of them. Adolescents may appear to forget the bond of childhood and challenge grandparents' value systems.

🍎 *Take comfort during this time in realizing that pulling away is a normal part of adolescent identity development.*

When adolescents reach young adulthood, they usually return to valuing their grandparents as well as grandparental insight, and the cross-generational bond becomes stronger than ever.

Love and Logic principles can assist grandparents in dealing with grandchildren at each of these life stages. Although the issues may change, the three basic principles remain constant. Remember to:

- ❖ Set enforceable limits
- ❖ Give choices
- ❖ Allow consequences with empathy

Love and Logic with Preschoolers. When it's nearly time to go and get groceries and a treat, Grandma can say,

---

LOVE AND LOGIC TIP 8
Setting Limits

Most people set limits on themselves. When they are unable to, but need to, limits must be set by others. To avoid limit-setting turning into a control battle, we can always give choices and allow consequences.

When limits must be set by a grandparent, it is best to talk them over in advance with your grandchild's parent(s) and obtain agreement for the consequence if the limit is broken. Involving your grandchild in limit-setting is also essential.

To ensure that the limits you are setting are effective, make certain that:

1. *The limit is definitely needed. Otherwise, why set it?*
2. *Consequences are possible.*
3. *Enforcement of the consequences will change the behavior.*

The most common mistakes grandparents make are setting limits that:

❖ They cannot enforce.
❖ Do not consider consequences in advance.
❖ Are too restrictive for the age of the child.
❖ Have not been approved by the grandchild's parents.

"My car leaves in five minutes." She doesn't tell four-year-old Johnny what to do, she simply tells him what she plans to do. If Johnny isn't ready, she calmly leaves without him, and he stays home with Grandpa. It usually doesn't take more than one time of missing a treat at the grocery store for Johnny to make a different decision the next time.

Being ready on time can also be handled with choices. When my wife and I (Foster) take our grandchildren with us in our car, they love to travel barefoot. In fact, the first sound we hear when they enter our vehicle is usually that of empty shoes thudding against the carpet.

When we are five minutes or so from the store, I say, "We're getting to the store in five minutes and you have some choices. You can wait in the car, you can go into the store barefoot, or you can put your shoes on now." We do not give them the option of our waiting for them to put on their shoes after we arrive. That, simply, is not an option. If we arrive and their shoes are not on, we ask, "Do you wish to go into the store barefoot or wait in the car?"

❧ *We remain in charge of our own time, and our grandchildren remain in charge of their own choices.*

Love and Logic with Grade Schoolers. When Tim was visiting his grandparents for a weekend, he showed up ready for church in a tacky pair of old boots instead of dress shoes. His grandfather was tempted to say, "Go change those before we leave." But he didn't. Instead, he left the choice up to his grandson. He said, "I wouldn't wear those boots to church, if I were you. I don't think they're appropriate. I'll leave the decision up to you, though."

Tim chose to wear the boots. After the service he returned to the car with a long face. His cousin had made fun of his boots. The next Sunday, Tim chose to wear his dress shoes. The lesson he learned about appropriate dressing was far better than the one he'd have learned had his grandfather insisted he wear dress shoes the week before.

❦ *When children make decisions based on their own choices, they learn lessons from the inside out.*

Love and Logic with Adolescents. When children reach adolescence, one of the most difficult issues can be back-talk.

❦ *Dealing with the fundamental issue of back-talk is essential, because it is important for children to learn the basic principle of treating others with respect.*

When Grandma asked Jill to help set the table for Sunday dinner, Jill said, "No! I need to call Sally on the phone. You do it!"

Grandma said, "Bad decision. I need to know that if I ask in a polite way, you'll respond in a polite way. I'll set the table alone. And I'll let you know how you can make this up to me later."

Grandma waited until the next time Jill needed a favor. Jill asked, "Grandma, can you drive me and Sally over to the mall at 2 o'clock?"

Grandma said, quietly, "Gee, Jill, I'm sorry. I used up that amount of time setting the dinner table for you last week. Please ask me again sometime when I haven't used my time doing your chores."

Solving Problems Without Creating Them

When Tim chose to wear tacky boots, Grandpa allowed this situation to remain Tim's problem and gave him an opportunity to learn from his choice. Grandma, on the other hand, provided consequences for Jill, because Jill's behavior also affected her.

❧ *The basic principle for a grandchild's behavior is: I don't have the right to create a problem for someone else in order to solve one of mine.*

This principle is good to use for all the relationships in our lives, no matter who is involved. When a child is disrespectful or obnoxious, we can calmly and warmly ask them to remove themselves from our presence. This is, after all, how we would treat any other human being.

Here's how I (Foster) like to think God sees the issue of respect. I think the reason he tells us not to take his name in vain is not because he has such a shaky self-image that he can't handle it, but rather because we need it for *our* self-image. Disrespect for him lowers *our* self-esteem. In the same way, allowing children to be disrespectful to us contributes to their own negative self-concept. When they learn to treat adults with respect, they grow up treating themselves with respect.

LOVE AND LOGIC TIP 9
Solving Problems Without Creating Problems

When I (Jim) was a grade-school principal, children sometimes forgot to take their lunches, permission slips, and tennis racquets to school. They telephoned their parents, who came running with the missing items. I did not approve. If they called their parents for forgotten items, I believed they were creating a problem for their parents, using parental time, gas and energy. So I made a rule. Students could use the school phone only if their call did not create a problem for someone else.

Eventually those children learned to solve their problems without creating more for their parents. They remembered what they needed for school. They also learned a basic principle of human relationships: I don't have the right to create a problem for someone else in order to solve one of mine.

We strongly recommend you remember that bonding with your grandchildren, whatever their age, includes:

1. Freely giving them your time
2. Providing them with focused, respectful attention
3. Using Love and Logic principles

We give this combination the highest grade for helping children become the best people they can be.

≈5≈

Building the
Three Generation Bond

If I chance to talk a little wild, forgive me;
I had it from my father.
—William Shakespeare, *Henry VIII*

A sk ten people you know this general question: Whose job is it to raise a child? And ten times out of ten you will hear an instant and automatic, "The parents' job, of course."

Parenting Today Requires More Involvement

In past decades, child rearing was often looked upon as the responsibility of parents *and* extended family members. With the breakdown of the extended family in recent generations, many mothers and fathers believe parenting today requires more of their involvement than raising children did in the past. Society agrees. The consensus is that parents should be the main, if not only, source of child discipline and guidance.

Out of Retirement

At a recent retirement home picnic I (Foster) saw several junior-high boys hassling retirement home residents who were using the outdoor rest room facilities. They knocked loudly on the walls when the rest rooms were in use and taunted the people inside. These days, obnoxious adolescent behavior in public goes on until the kids get bored with what they're doing. The adults, in most cases, shake their heads and mumble in frustration, "Kids nowadays . . . ," but do nothing more.

Not at this picnic. Without even conferring, several of the retired men approached the kids, intuitively making sure they outnumbered them. "Hey, guys," they said. "We don't like that, and we want it to stop. We'll give you a choice: Would you prefer to quit hassling us, or would you prefer to find your bodies in contact with the waste products in this building?"

LOVE AND LOGIC TIP 10
Dealing with Power Struggles

Power is a major issue between children and adults. While still very young, some kids realize they don't have much control over anything. A toddler thinks, "I'm the smallest. They tell me what to do, and I don't get to make decisions. I need to find a way to get some control." Then, winning the power struggle becomes all-important—more important than making good decisions.

When we offer kids a choice instead of making a demand, no power struggle ever begins. When we make a demand, we own the wise choice, leaving the child with only one way to win the power struggle—by making a foolish choice. Given a range of choices, a child has endless opportunities to choose wisely.

The kids chose to quit. In fact, they left—quickly and silently. No yelling. No hassling.

When we tell adults this story, most nod in approval. They like the actions those men took. But when those same adults are asked whose job it is to raise kids, they all answer, without hesitation, "The parents'."

They are right, for the most part. When it comes to raising kids, parents are in the driver's seat. They make thousands of decisions each day—about bedtime, mealtime manners, cleanup routines, schoolwork, chores. Parents are in charge of family policy. There are a few of us, however, from old-time America, who believe it is always appropriate for *any* person to calmly take the driver's seat when a child, or any other human being, chooses behavior that adversely affects us.

Grandma Grabs the Wheel

At Kevin's house, Grandpa and Grandma were visiting, and it was Kevin's bedtime. He said, "Aw, Mom, Grandpa and Grandma are here and I want to stay up later. There's no school tomorrow anyway. I can sleep in."

Grandma leaped in on his behalf, "It's okay, Mary. Just let him stay up. After all, we only get to visit here once in a blue moon."

Although Mary was driving, Grandma was grabbing the steering wheel. It's not appropriate for grandparents to drive from the passenger side. Sometimes you may serve as a map reader or navigator, but only in a situation that has been predetermined is it wise for you take a turn behind the wheel.

When Grandparents Should Act

There are four basic occasions that call for grandparents or other adults who are not parents to get involved in setting policy with children.

1. When a child's behavior directly affects you.

If a child's behavior has no impact on you, there is no problem. When it does, as in the case of the retirement group above, it is appropriate to act immediately.

LOVE AND LOGIC TIP 11
Punishment vs. Discipline

When a child misbehaves, an adult can decide to either punish or discipline. The purposes of these two actions are different, and so they produce different results.

	Punishment	**Discipline**
Purpose:	Punish the child's past behavior.	Shape the child's future decisions.
Techniques:	Isolation, time-out, withdrawal of privilege.	Isolation, time-out withdrawal of privilege.
Emotions:	Tension, frustration, rage, raised voices.	Disappointment, love and concern.
Results:	Child feels angry, out of control; feels loss of self-esteem; focuses on revenge, regaining control.	Child feels adults disappointment, concern; can focus on second-chance opportunities.

We punish a child for past choices; we discipline to shape future ones. Whereas punishment comes out of frustration and rage; discipline comes from love and concern. While both actions may use similar techniques—isolation, time-out, or withdrawal of a privilege—the emotional atmosphere of the two is different. The results? Find out for yourself. We find that discipline is the more effective choice every time.

In the following situation, Grandpa acted quickly and got to the root of the problem on the spot.

Kevin's Close Shave

Kevin, while his grandparents were visiting, took his grandfather's electric shaver from his suitcase and tried it out. Having no facial hair, he experimented on his arms, then left the hair-filled shaver on the floor of his room.

When Grandpa searched for and finally found his shaver the next morning, he said to Kevin, calmly but strongly, "My suitcase is private territory, and I don't like people using my shaver, especially without asking. I'm ready to shave, and I need a clean shaver, so I'd appreciate your removing your hair from this shaver so I can start clean. Here's a cleaning brush. I see you have a wastebasket over there. This is how you clean it."

After explaining the cleaning procedure, without doing the actual cleaning himself, Grandpa said, "When it's clean, please knock on the bathroom door and return it to me. Thanks, bud."

2. When a child's behavior violates Grandpa and Grandma's house rules.

On your home turf, you have the right to set the standards. My wife Hermie and I (Foster) are less lenient about children's clutter and mess than are our adult children. When our grandchildren visit, they adjust to our house rules. We expect them to put away their coats, boots, and toys after use.

Last Christmas, after an extended visit, we found candy wrappers tossed behind beds, atop counters, and

LOVE AND LOGIC TIP 12
A Sixty-second Scolding

A generation ago, scolding was the discipline of choice in most homes. A parent raised his or her voice, used a stern tone, addressed the guilty, and laid down the law for the future.

As a primary method of discipline, scolding is not especially effective. Used as an occasional tool in specific situations, scolding can be powerful. Surprisingly, it is not scolding itself that is effective, but, rather, scolding combined with love, consideration, and understanding.

A "Sixty-second Scolding" can be dramatically effective when:

1. a grandparent is in total control of his or her emotions
2. a grandparent has the consent of parents
3. used infrequently, and only with younger children
4. all other methods of problem-solving have been exhausted.

If these conditions have been met, here's how to do it.

Sixty-second Scolding

❖ Go directly to the child, look down into his or her eyeballs and say, "This is a behavior I will not tolerate." If necessary, be a little intimidating—bang on a nearby table.

❖ Then, drop to one knee, put an arm around the child and look lovingly into his or her eyes, and say, "The reason I'm telling you these things is that you are a kid who doesn't have to do this. You are a kid who knows how to be great. I want you to know how much I appreciate you when you behave like the terrific kid I know you really are." Then give the child a hug.

The ideal ending is the child bursting into tears, hugging you back and saying, "I know. I'm sorry." Life, however, does not always have ideal endings, so if a sixty-second scolding is used once and is not effective, it should never be used again. If it is effective, use it like spice—just an occasional sprinkling, as needed, when other discipline methods have failed.

under chairs. On their next visit, we said, "Kids, these candy jars stay out just as long as the wrappers go in the wastebasket. If we find wrappers trashed on the floors and behind furniture, we'll need to put away the candy jars." We set the rule *before* any wrappers got tossed again.

Sometimes grandchildren may protest a rule: "At home we don't have to put things away." When this happens, it isn't necessary to criticize their parents or defend your reason for your standards. You can simply say, "I understand that's how things are at home, but you're in Grandma's house now. At Grandma's house, we go by Grandma's rules."

You can even go one step further and say, "I'm looking forward to the time when you're grown up and I come and visit you at *your* house. I guarantee you, at your house, I will follow your house rules."

3. When parents are not present.

In many instances, parents are not present, and grandparents become parent figures. Should this happen to you, you will want to be prepared to set limits for behavior and respond immediately to misbehavior.

Heather's Deep Pockets

Grandpa Vic took his five-year-old granddaughter Heather shopping. After they left a department store, Vic noticed Heather's two coat pockets were bulging and saw an unpurchased candy bar in each one.

"What's in your pocket, Heather?" he asked.

"Candy bars. I found them just lying there," Heather said.

Vic spoke with love and logic: "You know, Heather, when you find something in a store, it belongs to the store," said Vic. "If you take it, that's called stealing, which is not a good thing to do. Show me where you found them."

Vic and Heather reentered the store, and Heather showed him. "Taking a candy bar from a store is the same as taking money from them, because they paid for the candy bars. The candy bars belong to them," said Vic. "We need to find the owner so you can give them back, explain what you did, and tell her you're sorry."

When they found the manager, Vic let Heather do the talking. Heather's voice quivered and her eyes were wet, but she took responsibility for her action. "I took these candy bars, and I am very sorry," she said.

When Vic returned Heather home that day, he said nothing until Heather had gone out to the swing set. Then he briefly told Heather's parents what had happened. Because Vic had been alone with Heather, he took responsibility for disciplining her.

4. If a parent has agreed that a grandparent may take action.

Good grandparenting, when relating to your adult children, lies in being overt and up-front rather than covert and devious. If, for example, your grandchild pulls your cat's tail while he and his mother are visiting, and you find yourself wincing—later, when you are alone with his mother, you may wish to tell her, "I'm not comfortable when Robert pulls Tuffy's tail . . . and neither is Tuffy. Would you mind if I say something to him about that?"

LOVE AND LOGIC TIP 13
Time-out

A time-out deprives a child of the positive stimulation of being around adults or other children. It's a good way to encourage appropriate behavior, because it generates thinking on the part of the child at a time when he or she is alone. We do not need to pronounce time-outs in a stern voice. We can simply say, "You may come back when you can be sweet—very sweet."

If we are gentle and consistent, time-outs will mold a child and motivate him or her to behave appropriately.

Some parents may respond by saying, "Sure, fine. If you see something that bothers you, speak up!" Others may say, "If you want to follow-up or back up something I say, that's fine, but I'd rather not have you say something before I do." Or a parent might respond, "No, if something needs to be said, when we're all together I will say it." It's beyond the scope of this book to analyze why a parent would insist that something be said only when everyone is together. This type of answer is rooted in his or her own personal problems. Failure to acknowledge their wishes in these situations could lead to more problems.

❦ *The point to remember is that you want to work with your children, not against them.*

Grandparents can make clear that, when all three generations are together, they do not want to create stress in their relationship with their son or daughter by overstepping their bounds. Perhaps they can set up a mutually agreed-upon signal. Grandpa may say, "I really don't have a clear sense of when you think I'm invading your parental territory. When you feel that's happening, please tug on your right earlobe and I'll back off. If you're not tugging, I'll assume I'm on safe ground."

Out of the Mouth of Jane

John is a grandfather who is sensitive to this issue. He was visiting his daughter and granddaughter Jane one evening. When Jane's mother asked her to help clear the table after dinner, Jane said, "I don't have to do that. You're always making me work. Other kids' moms don't make them work, and I'm not going to be a slave in this house."

John remained silent as Jane stormed to her room. His daughter said, "I don't know what I'm going to do with her. I'm at my wit's end."

John said, "I know. Handling kids can be tough."

As they stacked plates and rinsed silverware, he and his daughter talked about her new job, the state of the divorce proceedings, and how her car was running, but they did not discuss Jane's behavior any further.

Several days later, over lunch, John said, "You know, I've been thinking about Jane. It hurts me to see her mouthing off to you that way. Would you like my support at times like that? If so, let's decide what that support should look like."

The two of them agreed that he could discuss Janes's disrespectful behavior when just the two of them were together.

A few days later, over sodas with Jane, Grandpa said, "You know, I've noticed you mouthing off to your mom a lot lately. I know you're hurting. Your mom's hurting, too. Because of the changes in your household right now, she's doing double duty with her new job. You might want to think about making things easier for her and helping lighten her load a bit."

Pointing to a parent's workload and pain can be more effective coming from a third party than from the parent. A child sees the assessment as more objective and, therefore, more valid.

5. When parents have forfeited their rights.

The less responsibility parents take in training and caring for their children, the more active and responsible grandparents tend to become. Sometimes parents give up their responsibility entirely, and grandparents take on the steering wheel of parenting and discipline. In essence, they *become* parents.

This is a complex issue that has many ramifications. In Chapter 9, When You're Thinking About Raising Your Grandchild, we elaborate more fully the steps you can take in making this enormous decision.

Resolving Gift, Money and Time Conflicts

We've discussed setting standards and grandparents getting involved in discipline and family policy. But the job of raising kids requires more than policy. It requires time and money.

Whose time? Whose money? The answer to these questions is usally the same as for policy: "The parents'." But neat and tidy, square-cornered responses don't always fit into the circle of life.

Two of grandparents' greatest joys are visiting and giving gifts to their grandchildren. Until now, you may have taken these simple acts for granted. We want to help you make certain that the gift-giving and visiting you are doing is not a source of conflict within your family structure.

On the other hand, there are times when grandparents are asked to do and give more than they would like. We want to assist you with that issue as well by helping you understand how to set limits.

GIFT-GIVING

Giving gifts to grandchildren is many grandparents' greatest joy. They see the child rejoice in receiving and using what they've given. These gifts are mortar for the bond.

A gift need not be large or expensive in order to be appropriate.

Triceratops

One set of grandparents we know buys triceratops memorabilia for their four-year-old granddaughter Sarah—triceratops gummy bears, triceratops erasers, triceratops shoe laces. The reason? Sarah figured out her own little pun to make triceratops her special animal. She explained it to her grandmother. "Get it, Grandma? Listen hard! It's a try-sarah-tops." Grandma was hooked, and triceratops trinkets have been coming Sarah's way on special occasions ever since.

How can grandparents decide on the amount of their gift-giving? How can they tell if a particular gift is on safe ground? Here is a three-part test to assist you.

You are doing appropriate gift-giving when:

1. Grandchildren do not look at your gifts with a sense of entitlement.

If, when you appear for a visit, the first thing your grandchild asks is, "What did you bring me?" that child is beginning to feel he or she is "entitled" to receive something from you every time you visit.

2. Grandchildren value your gifts.

If, thirty seconds after a gift is opened a grandchild drops it on the carpet, forgets it, and never looks at it again, you may need to reevaluate your gift-giving.

3. Your grandchildren's parents approve.

Tension may arise when parents think grandparents give their children too much, or when grandparents give gifts parents believe are not proper. If you sense that your son or daughter is uncomfortable with your gift-giving, it's time to be up front and ask during a quiet moment for some feedback:

❖ "I'd like to know how you feel about the things I've been giving Tommy. I value your opinion and I'd like to know if you see them as appropriate."
❖ "Are the gifts at the right age level?"
❖ "Would you like to see them more or less frequently?"

When your son or daughter responds, follow active listening techniques:

Listen
Check if you understand
Respond

An active listening response might be:

❖ "I see. In other words, I need to consult you more about the gifts."
❖ "Ah-hah, so you wish I could spend more time with the kids?"

Never ask these questions unless you are willing to listen and deal with the response.

GETTING TO SEE GRANDCHILDREN

Grandparents may sometimes wish for more time with grandchildren than is available to them. John, for example, lives across the state from his grandchildren, and sees them one week each year on their family vacation. Penny's grandchildren, who live just across town, come for Sunday dinner less and less frequently. When grandparents want to see their children and grandchildren more often, approaching them with demands generally does nothing more than make things worse.

There's a difference between making a demand and asking for what you would like. There's nothing wrong with expressing needs and wishes.

Free to Frolic

When Art and Penny wanted to see more of their grandchildren, they said to their children, "We really care about those kids and we'd like to see them a little more often. Is there anything we can do to make it easier on you for us to get together with them? We could take them for a weekend and we could meet you at a mid-point if the drive is too long."

Their children said they would think it over and get back to them, but three months passed and they didn't respond. Penny and Art suspected that transportation might not be the underlying cause for their ongoing separation. Perhaps there was an unspoken reason preventing their children from being up front with them.

They tried a new tactic. Penny said, "We're wondering if there is anything we do that makes parenting more difficult for you. Are we saying or doing something that's giving your kids ideas you would rather they not have? Are you afraid they'll be too hard for us to handle?"

Art and Penny learned that day that their children were afraid of what their grandchildren would do in a home furnished with Victorian antiques. Perhaps they would break something valuable, or dirty a precious rug. Being the creative grandparents they are, now, several weekends each year, they take their grandchildren camping. They rent a tent and camping equipment and head for a national park where the kids are free to frolic without the worry of breaking antiques.

When children are hesitant to let their own kids visit more often with the kids' grandparents, there are reasons. Generally, they fall into one of two categories: A logistical problem, which you may be able to help solve;

or, an unspoken reason in the parents' minds. When grandparents ask questions and express their wishes, they are, more often than not, able to negotiate an arrangement that will satisfy all three generations.

SETTING LIMITS

Sometimes, the shoe is on the other foot. Instead of wanting less time and money spent with and on grandchildren, adult children want more. These are times that call for setting limits.

Child Care for Jerry's Kids

When Jerry's wife Gina left him three months ago, Jerry, who has two preschool kids and a full-time job, asked Grandpa and Grandma to care for the kids while he went to work. When it began to look as if Gina and Jerry would not get back together, and that this child-care arrangement was going to be permanent, Grandpa and Grandma were uncertain how to act. Whose job is it to provide child care for Jerry's kids?

Food for Sally's Grandkids

When Sally stopped by her daughter's apartment to see her eight-and ten-year-old grandchildren after school last year, she opened the refrigerator to find a few crusts of bread. The cupboards had only one box of dry cereal. Horrified, she took them to the grocery store and they pushed the cart while she bought milk, bread, peanut butter, apples, oranges, and carrots.

The next week, the refrigerator had no bread and the cereal was gone from the cupboard, so she bought again. That was a month ago. It didn't take long for her grandkids to come to rely on Grandma to buy groceries.

This was a problem for Grandma, however, because her budget began to stretch a trifle thin. Whose job is it to provide food for these kids?

Education for Randy

Randy plans to go to college, but his parents don't have the finances to fund his education. His folks have been hinting around for months about their lack of finances. They even mentioned that one of Randy's friend's grandparents is funding each grandchild's college education. The pressure is on Randy's grandparents to fork up the funding. Randy's grandfather Ken asks: Whose job is it to fund Randy's education?

In these cases, parents expect more from grandparents than gifts and visits.

🍎 *Researchers have discovered that parents who were rescued in their own childhood are likely to expect or need rescuing for their children.*

If parents have high expectations for child care and financial support, it can be helpful to examine family patterns. The parent who expects these, or demands these, or slyly manipulates to get these, is often the grown-up product of helicopter parenting. He or she probably was consistently rescued from tight corners as a child and follows that pattern as an adult.

Grandma Sally will probably continue to provide groceries unless she chooses to change the pattern. Randy's parents will accept grandparents' college financing and could easily miss the application deadline for financial aid again next year.

A crucial question here is whether you, as a grandparent, wish to continue rescuing your children. One thing you can be sure of:

❦ *Irresponsible parents will allow you to play the role of rescuer, and will beg you to play it, just as long as you are willing.*

Coming to Terms

There are two fundamental principles to watch for when dealing with parents who have high expectations for child care or financial assistance from you:

❖ The best agreements are overt and up front, rather than covert and unspoken. Child care and financial arrangements should come through the front door rather than the back door.
❖ Agreements need a plan and may call for a specified time frame. Family crises can turn temporary arrangements into permanent ones—often, against your wishes. Don't let a crisis keep you from discussing your hidden needs.

The Love and Logic procedure to follow in dealing with these issues is:

1. *Listen.* Ask parents to tell you what their hopes and thoughts are about your care or financial support of your grandchild.

2. *Show you understand.* Tell parents in your own words what you hear them saying their hopes are.

3. *Allow yourself time to think.* There are two magic sentences to use when dealing with parents' expectations of grandparents. We wish we could install them permanently in the human consciousness grandparent memory bank—in large letters. Those sentences are:

"I'll think it over."
"I'll get back to you on it."

These are simple sentences with dynamic power. The reason? Kids of rescuing parents learn young that if they can hit their parents with a request when the parents are frazzled or off guard, they can probably get more from them. This is a lesson they don't forget as adults. It is the wise grandparent who allows her- or himself time to think over a decision.

4. *Consider the needs of each generation involved.* There are three generations of needs to consider here: grandchild, parent, and grandparent. Remember to factor in your own wants and needs when considering options.

5. *When you tell them your decision, explain, "I've thought it over, and what will work for me is . . . "* The words, "what will work for me," may well be some of the most valuable words grandparents can use. Learn them well.

It is important to explain in "I-statements," without accusation, blame, or restrictions for the other person's behavior. "I-statements" tell the listener how the *speaker* feels or plans to act, rather than how the listener should feel or act.

6. *If necessary, be a broken record.* If the parent says, "But that's not fair . . . ," simply reply, "That could be. I understand that's how you feel about this. What will work for me, however, is . . ." and repeat your previous statement. Do the same for each objection raised.

LOVE AND LOGIC TIP 14
"I-Statements"

"I-statements" are very powerful tools that may be used with both children and adults. To send an "I-statement," you tell your listener how *you* are feeling, the action that provoked that feeling, and the effect of that action on you. An adult, confronting a child about lying may say, "Honey, I feel upset when you don't tell me the truth, because then I'm uncertain whether or not to believe you when you tell me other things."

An "I-statement" presents the speaker's feelings and responses in a way that cannot be contradicted by the listener. It does not make accusations or tell the listener what to do.

The proper use of "I-statements" takes a little work. The adult who mistakes the following statement for an "I-statement" still needs a little practice: "I feel angry when you act so stupid because you impress everybody as being dumb."

This statement begins by expressing a feeling, but then it becomes judgmental ("You act so stupid") and makes a statement the listener can take issue with ("You impress everyone as being dumb").

When I (Foster) first heard of "I-statements," I thought, "What a wimpy way to talk! They will never work." I was shocked to discover that they work with most people most of the time. They work because they imply that the listener:

1. Can figure out his or her own solution.
2. Does not need to be told what to do.
3. Cares about other people's feelings.
4. Is intelligent and can figure out a thoughtful response.
5. Will not argue, because there is nothing to debate.

Using these principles and procedures, let's look at the families we used as examples and find out how they handled their situations.

A Return to Child Care for Jerry's Kids

Jerry's mother, Kate, had been caring for his two preschoolers for three months, since Gina, his wife, left him. One afternoon when he came to pick them up, Kate and Jerry sat down and had a cup of coffee while the kids played in the next room.

Kate began, "Jerry, I know that your life has been topsy-turvy the past three months and you may not be looking very far ahead at this point. I'd appreciate having some sense of what you're thinking about for long-term care of Lisa and Barry. I'm not really sure what you have in mind."

Jerry looked at his mom in surprise. "I've been in such a fog, I haven't really thought about it, Mom. I guess I assumed it would go on like this—but that might not be fair to you and dad. It's up to you, I guess, but I'd appreciate it if they could spend some days with you."

Kate said, "You'd like them to spend some days here, but you won't be hurt if we can't watch them full-time?"

"That's right, Mom."

"I'll think it over. I'll get back to you on it in a few days."

The next week Kate told him she'd love to have the kids each Tuesday and Thursday. Jerry found a child-care center for his kids the other three days.

A Return to Food for Sally's Grandkids

After a month of buying groceries, Sally realized she was caught in a trap, unless she took action. She invited her daughter Pat to lunch while the children were at school. Over soup and sandwiches, she said, "Pat, I'm concerned about the food situation for you and the kids. You know I've been buying groceries for the past month. Well, my food budget is getting stretched a little thin. I'm wondering what your thinking is about providing food for the kids?"

Pat attacked. "I don't see how your food budget can be stretched that thin. You and dad have twice the money I do, and you could help out a lot more than you actually do!"

Sally checked it out. "So you're thinking that you'd like us to continue stocking your cupboard for the girls? How long are you thinking you'd like us to do that for?"

Pat said, "As long as they need it. Good grief, here I am working a minimum wage job, which barely covers the cost of gas and cigarettes, and you're expecting me to make it pay for food too? It can't be done. Besides, working the long hours I do, I don't have time to constantly be running to the grocery store."

Sally said, "So you're thinking that we should provide groceries for the girls until they're grown."

"I guess that's about it, yeah."

Sally said, "I'll think that over and I'll get back to you."

A few days later, Sally talked with Pat. "I've thought it over, and what I'm willing to do is to buy groceries for one more month. That will give you time to do some financial planning, if you want."

Pat attacked again. "You don't love your grandchildren. Do you want them to go hungry?" To each attack, Sally responded, "I understand that's how you feel about this. A month of groceries is what I am willing to do."

Sally was taking steps to abandon her role as rescuing parent, and placing the responsibility back on Pat's shoulders.

Asking her daughter to find a solution put the responsibility back where it belonged. In this way, Sally wound up being far more helpful to her daughter in the long run. By not rescuing her, Sally encouraged her daughter to learn what she needed to do to help herself.

A Return to Randy's Education

After listening to hints for several months, Randy's grandparents asked their children about their expectations. "We know that you're concerned about Randy's college education, and we sense you'd like us to help out. We'd like to know what your thoughts are about this."

Randy's parents responded, "We can't afford to pay for Randy's college education, but we know that you can. Since he's your grandchild, we think you should."

Grandpa Ken asked, "How much are you thinking of per year? And are you thinking of it for just the first year, or for the full four years?"

Costs came to about $15,000 per year, and yes, they were thinking of all four years.

Grandpa said, "Let us think about that. We'll get back to you on it."

Later, he told them, "We've talked about it, and I'd like my grandchildren to know that I value education, and I certainly value theirs. What I'm able to do for each of my ten grandchildren is this. I'll provide a $500 high school graduation gift, to be used at the college of their choice for each of my grandchildren."

His children were shocked. They said, "That's just a drop in the bucket. We'll never be able to afford Randy's college."

Grandpa said, "That may be. Still, $500 is what I'm able to provide."

They said, "Our friends' parents fund full tuition." He answered, "That may be. And $500 is what I'm able to provide."

By openly discussing expectations and sensitivities to them, Kate, Sally, and Ken have begun healthy patterns of behavior with their children and grandchildren by making overt agreements, in advance, rather than letting a pattern emerge without discussion or planning. They've clarified their boundaries and limits and have found all-important responses to the question, "Whose job is it to raise this child?"

❖ ❖ ❖

Congratulations! You have just completed your first steps in learning Love and Logic principles for grandparents. We hope that you have found the introductory chapters insightful and promising for the relationships you hold dear to you.

In Chapters 6 through 10 that follow, we go into greater detail about specific problems we have discovered to be prevalent in many homes around the country: when grandparents and parents disagree, when a grandchild's parents divorce, when your family includes step-grandchildren, deciding to raise your grandchild, and grandparents-too-soon. It is possible that the spe-

BUILDING THE THREE GENERATION BOND

cific problems addressed in these chapters do not fit
your particular situation. You are welcome to read them
for any insights that might prove helpful, or to pass
over them to Chapter 11, where, Love and Logic principles are reviewed, and to Part II, which contains
Pearls we hope will prove helpful to you.

Often the presence of a grandchild in the family will
trigger or resolve old problems. The outcome relies on
how everyone handles the situation. As a Love and
Logic grandparent, you have the opportunity to help
make the situation a positive one.

≈6≈

When Grandparents
And Parents Disagree

*We don't see things as they are;
we see them as we are."*
—Anaïs Nin

Gertrude Bites Her Lip

Gertrude was visiting her daughter over a mid-afternoon cup of coffee when Sandra came home from school, threw her coat on the floor, flopped her books on the table, grabbed a snack, and headed for her room. Her mother stopped her in the hallway in an instant.

"Sandra, you get back here right now and put your coat and books where they belong!"

Gertrude watched in silence, biting her lip. She wanted to tell her daughter about the importance of offering choices rather than making threats, but didn't know if she should.

Safe Thoughts for Don's Grandson

Don's grandson is fifteen. His parents just got a school permit for him to drive. He lives in a busy city where driving is not easy, and Grandpa and Grandma worry about his safety. They also wonder about their right to express their own opinion. After all, parents, not grandparents, are in charge.

Taking Account of Julie

Julie returned to work six weeks after her daughter

LOVE AND LOGIC TIP 15
Choices vs. Threats

Threats work for some kids, but for many they fail. Why? When someone threatens Sandy the first thing Sandy thinks is, "She can't make me do that." Her second thought is, "But maybe she can." An internal dialogue begins. "No, she can't." "Yes, she can." "No . . . " Soon the dialogue becomes an internal argument. Sandy gets angry and resentful. She becomes either passive-aggressive or passive-resistive.

If she becomes passive-aggressive, she hurts you back, sometimes so subtly you don't even know it's revenge. When her teacher refuses to answer Sandy's tenth unnecessary question about an assignment she made her do, Sandy says, "My mom says good teachers make sure a kid knows what she's doing before doing an assignment." Or Sandy "accidentally" breaks one of her grandmother's dishes to get back at Grandma for threats made to get Sandy to wash them.

If Sandy responds to threats in a passive-resistive way, she resists without letting you know she's resisting. When Sandy's teacher tells her to come into the classroom, her body may move in low gear. At home she she might wash the dishes, but leave the sink full of dirty water and the counters unwashed.

The threat cycle is easily avoided by offering choices instead of making demands.

---

was born. Her job as an account executive, which is very demanding, often requires her to put in 50–60 hours per week. Grandma wishes she would stay home and take care of her newborn. She believes preschool years are important and that an at-home mom is ideal for her granddaughter. She's not sure that the baby-sitter Julie has chosen is really committed to providing quality care for children.

Francine as Role Model

Francine's boyfriend just moved in. She is a single mother of a ten-year-old and a twelve-year-old. Her parents wince at the impact this might have on her children and the kind of role model this provides for them.

Once grown children have established their own families, they set up lifestyles and parenting policies that may differ from those they grew up with in their parents' home. Some of their choices meet with grandparents' approval and some don't.

Three Commandments for Smooth Relationships

When grandparents and parents disagree, we believe it's time to look at the three Love and Logic commandments for smooth relationships between them:

1. Do not issue orders.

"Francine, your boyfriend has simply got to move out. Besides being immoral, it's terrible for your kids."

2. Do not play martyr and whine.

"How can you let Don drive at that age? We couldn't stand it if he were seriously hurt in a car accident."

3. Do not give advice without permission.

LOVE AND LOGIC TIP 16
Thinking Words and Fighting Words

In many families, setting limits means issuing commands. Love and Logic families do something different. They ask questions and offer choices, which places the responsibility for decision-making on the children.

Love and Logic families help kids do exactly what we want them to do: Think—as much as possible. When children choose an option, *they* do the thinking. This makes the choice stick with them. Note the difference between fighting and thinking words in the examples that follow. Say them out loud; practice them with your spouse so you can hear what your grandchild will hear.

Fighting Words:	"Be nice to each other. Quit fighting."
Thinking Words:	"You guys are welcome to come back as soon as you work that out."
Fighting Words:	"It's cold outside. Put on your coat."
Thinking Words:	"Would you like to wear your coat or carry it?"
Fighting Words:	"You better get going on your homework right now."
Thinking Words:	"Feel free to join us for some television when your studying is done."

"Honey, if you'd like a little advice, I just read this wonderful book on parenting, and it says giving orders stifles kids' ability to grow up responsible. There's a better way to do it. . . ."

In one survey of parents, unwanted advice was listed as the main cause of irritation with grandparents, but all three of these situations come up in most families at one time or another. The basic rule of the road for grandparents, when they disagree with parents on how to raise children, is this:

🍎 *Parents are the drivers behind the steering wheel. Grandparents never grab the wheel, unless they have parents' permission.*

House Rules

Grandparents should have their own rules. They have a right to different house rules. House rules disagreements are some of the simplest to deal with once everyone has been made aware of them and grandchildren are properly prepared for them.

It may prove advantageous to have a brief, all-inclusive, three-generation discussion, at which the rules are set with your grandchildren:

1. At Grandpa and Grandma's house, you go by their rules; at your parents' house, you go by your parents' rules.

2. At home you may wear your shoes as you walk indoors; at Grandpa's house you remove them on the porch.

3. At home you may play with all the dolls, but at Grandma's house you may not touch Grandma's antique doll collection in the living room. Some dolls are for playing with, and others are for looking at.

4. On a family trip to the store, Mom and Dad will wait for you to put your shoes on when you get to the parking lot; Grandpa and Grandma want you to have your shoes on when you arrive if you wish to go into the store with them.

5. At Grandma's house you may take a cookie from the cookie jar when you wish; at home, you need to ask permission.

These differences in house rules are not confusing for children. They adapt amazingly well to differing expectations in differing situations. Young children learn quickly that different friends have different expectations. Junior-high students must adapt their behavior to five or six different teachers, and they do so without blinking an eye or breaking stride. Kids are adaptable and flexible people.

A Four-Step Approach to Differences

If you are uncomfortable with differences in house rules, you may wish to discuss them with your children. "Our cookie jar is always open to your kids, and we'd like to know if you are comfortable with that." If parents are uncomfortable, you may need to negotiate an acceptable compromise. "We could close the cookie jar an hour before each meal."

It is important to remember, of course, not to be critical of parents' policies. If a grandchild calls a difference in policies to your attention, you can simply say, "We're at Grandma's house now, and here we go by Grandma's rules."

❧ *Refraining from criticizing parents is important in all situations, even when you think parents are dead wrong.*

To criticize a child's parents in his presence is to wound that child. It is easy for your grandchild to conclude that if you are critical of his parents in their absence, you are likely to be critical of him when he is gone.

When parents are present you can disagree with them in a grandchild's presence about anything— the best presidential candidate, the relative merits of Fords and Chevys, the best policy for winning a game of Rook, or the usefulness of the American welfare system. You can debate whether to have ham or turkey for Thanksgiving dinner, the value (or lack of value) of this season's TV shows, and whether or not "bleaken" is a valid Scrabble entry.

❧ *However, in the presence of a child you cannot disagree with parents on how they are handling that child.*

Driving lessons don't work well when children are passengers in the car. They are best saved for times when you and a parent are alone. The timing of your discussion with parents is also important. The best time is not immediately after your son has exploded at your grandson and told him he was a good-for-nothing who would never amount to anything. A better time is several days later when the two of you have golfed nine holes and are settling in for a soft drink at the clubhouse. Everyone is more calm and objective. Even then, you need permission to give a driving lesson. You don't want to just grab the wheel and leap into a lecture. You want to make sure your child is ready to listen.

When you disagree with how your son or daughter is parenting, the following four-step Love and Logic approach can be effective:

1. Question
2. Listen
3. Understand
4. Ask permission

QUESTION

Problem-solving often works best when it begins with a question. You are showing concern rather than making a demand. That question can include some expressed concern for the well-being of both parent and child.

❦ *Your intention in asking the question must be to understand and to get clarification—not to express judgment.*

In some cases, it's important to validate the emotion a parent experiences, even when you do not approve of the behavior that parent has exhibited.

Gertrude Validates, Then Questions

After watching her daughter explode at Sandra on several occasions, Gertrude picked a quiet moment and observed, "I was sad for you and Sandra yesterday when she came home. You seemed really frustrated with her."

Sandra's mom said, "I just don't know how to handle her anymore. She acts like home is just a place to trash, and the rest of us exist just to meet her needs. She doesn't listen to a word I say . . . "

When her daughter's voice trailed off, Gertrude said, "That must really be hard. Does she listen any better when you give stern orders?"

Gertrude validated her daughter's emotion and followed it with a question.

LISTEN

Listening is a priceless treasure given freely to another person without charge. Good listening is more than slumping in the presence of another person with an ear on each side of your skull. Listening is showing interest. Nodding that you understand. Looking into the eyes of the other person and showing acceptance, rather than staring at the floor in embarrassment.

Gertrude Listens

When Gertrude asked if yelling was effective, her daughter answered, "Not, really. It used to be, but lately it does nothing but wear out my voice. I don't know what else to do. I'm so frustrated. I don't think I should be responsible for picking up after her. She needs to learn to pull her own weight. She's at a difficult age. She used to be so easy. Suddenly in the past year she's like a different person."

Gertrude didn't interrupt. Coffee mug cradled in her hands, leaning forward, she kept her eyes on her daughter and nodded as her daughter spoke. Gertrude listened.

CHECK YOUR UNDERSTANDING

Each of us has a filter between our ears and our brain, and what we hear is often slightly different from what was said. As Anaïs Nin said, "We don't see things as they are; we see them as we are." Understanding can be verified by restating what you have just heard. The question form works well.

Gertrude Checks Her Understanding

Gertrude said, "It sounds like Sandra is becoming less compliant, and you're hurt and frustrated by it—especially when it comes to her picking up after herself and being responsible at home. Are you feeling helpless, because what used to work with her doesn't work anymore?"

Her daughter said, "Yeah, Mom, and I really don't like yelling at her, but I don't know what else to do anymore."

Gertrude was tempted to leap in with information about an adolescent's drive toward independence, the need for power and control over one's own life, and the value of choices, but she thought of step four and held her tongue. She asked permission.

LOVE AND LOGIC TIP 17
Gaining Control by Giving Some Away

Magically, giving a child choices and ownership of his or her decisions actually gives an adult more control. Why? Because a child who has no control over his life is a child who will spend nearly 100 percent of his time trying to get it. These are the kids who work to manipulate adults and the system as well.

A child with some control over his or her life will spend little time trying to gain more. That's why this paradox is true: Adults gain control by giving some of it away!

GET PERMISSION TO GIVE ADVICE

Getting permission to make suggestions can be done as a statement or as a question. A grandparent can say, "Would you be interested in hearing some of my thoughts on that?" A statement can be a little more subtle. A grandparent could say, "If you'd be interested in hearing some ideas on that sometime, let me know."

❦ *If permission is not granted, it's important to bow out graciously. The way you leave a situation is the way it will be remembered.*

If a parent says, no, that parent does not want to hear your ideas at that time. You need to accept that.

"That's all right," you can say. "I understand that you need to raise Johnny your way. He's your son, not mine, and I know that."

If you close the conversation in a huff, "Well, I really would have wished for more wisdom on your part, but I guess I have no control," your huffiness is what will leave a lasting impression and be remembered most vividly.

Gertrude Asks Permission

When her daughter said she was out of alternatives, Gertrude said, "If you like, I could give that some thought, ask a few people I know, and see if I can come up with some ideas for you."

Her daughter looked up and said, "Sure, I'm willing to try anything at this point."

Gertrude said, "I'll get back to you on it next week."

Gertrude wanted to think through her suggestions,

and she did want to check with a few friends, before making suggestions to her daughter.

A few days later she suggested several options:

1. "An enforceable statement might work, if you position yourself between Sandra and the refrigerator when she comes in the door. You could say, 'I notice you like to have a snack after school, and that's great. Feel free to open the refrigerator just as soon as your clothes are hung up.'"

2. "Offering choices might be another approach. Some parents offer their kids the choice of putting away their things before they eat, or having their parent put them away and the kid then doing a household chore the parent doesn't enjoy doing in exchange. They ask the child to think it over and get back to them in the morning with their decision."

3. "A third choice might be to demonstrate what happens when no one does their chores. Discuss with Sandra that you both seem to be tired of doing your household chores, and you'll try two weeks of neither of you doing them. Sandra might find out, after a few days, that she's better off picking up after herself so Mom can continue cooking and driving her to soccer practice."

In any situation, if a parent shuts the door, the grandparent needs to find a more exciting topic of conversation immediately. If a parent opens the door, the grandparent can follow with listening, checking under-

LOVE AND LOGIC TIP 18
Turning Your Words into Gold

Our words can be either garbage or gold in a child's life. The garbage variety are idle, useless words that tell someone else what to do, yet give us no power to enforce them. Although these statements may be based on positive principles, they do not produce positive results.

Garbage statements:
- "Save your money."
- "Talk to me with respect."

"Gold" statements are based on positive principles, but show empathy and encourage children to think and work things out for themselves. Their power lies in putting the responsibility where it belongs—on the person with the problem—while showing that you care.

Gold statements:
- "I'm sorry you're out of money. I don't have any more jobs for you at the moment, but when the lawn needs mowing again, I'll let you know.
- "Feel free to talk to me when you can do it with appropriate words and a gentler tone of voice. I'll be glad to listen then."

standing, and asking permission to give advice. It's all love and logic, and we've seen it work.

Making Peace With Your Parenting History

LEARNING TO ACCEPT

Grandparents sometimes wrestle with their responsibility for the way their children parent today. One grandpa we know, Jack, believes his son is very harsh with his children—a drill sergeant, who says to his kids, "I don't care how you feel. I want it done and I want it done now." Jack has mellowed over the years, and now takes a more consultant approach in dealing with his son and other people. In his son, however, Jack sees echoes of his own parenting.

Linda's daughter Sue takes very little responsibility for her children. Sue takes Linda's child care for granted, and expects Linda to baby-sit them at a moment's notice. Sue once dropped them off and went off on a week's trip with her boyfriend. Linda came home to find her grand-kids on her front doorstep with a note pinned to their shirts telling her when her daughter would be back. Linda had been a helicopter parent, constantly rescuing her daughter, giving her very little responsibility. Now her daughter expects the same rescuing in her adult life.

Both Jack and Linda experience parental guilt. Both see the effects of their parenting in the way *their* children are parenting. They know they've made mistakes, and they need to work toward acceptance of their own mistakes as well as the impact of those mistakes on their son and daughter.

Sometimes a parent of an adult child sits in my (Foster's) office and says, "I just can't accept this." Sometimes "this" is a daughter pregnant out of wedlock, or a divorce or desertion. In reality, though, we must accept it. What other option is there?

LEARNING TO CHANGE

Acceptance, however is different from approval. Just because you continue to accept the person, does not mean you approve of the person's behavior.

❦ To accept is to come to an emotional peace with a circumstance you are unable to change.

We can, gradually and sometimes painfully, come to accept our past parenting mistakes—pick up the pieces and go on. We don't, however, have to continue to make the same mistakes. Linda does not need to continue to rescue her daughter, just because she played the rescuer when her daughter was a child and because she blames herself for her daughter's irresponsibility. To do so is to perpetuate the mistake and continue to face the same behavior.

Jack doesn't order his son to stop giving orders, although the drill sergeant in him might be tempted to do so. Instead, he becomes a model of the consultant approach. Perhaps he also tries a little heart-to-heart with his son. Heart-to-hearts can work with sons as well as with grandsons.

Remember that a heart-to-heart is short, sweet, and ends with a question. It doesn't help to tell drivers with a decade of experience that the driving lessons you gave them were all wrong. But an occasional question about the possible results of running stop signs might correct some bad habits without lessons.

Jack might approach the subject with his son over a soft drink or beer some afternoon by saying, "You know, when I raised you, I thought I knew all the answers, and I think I ordered you around a lot. I remember you telling me you were never going to be like that. Do you ever say something these days to your kids and hear my voice coming out of your mouth?"

Then Jack can wait and see where his son takes the conversation. He isn't going to change a decades-old pattern in one little conversation, and he knows it.

On another occasion he might ask, "Do you ever worry that your kids might feel the same way about you that you felt about me?" And still later he might say, "I've got a tape called *Helicopters, Drill Sergeants, and Consultants* that you might enjoy. Don't listen to it, though, unless you're in a mood to laugh."

Linda might choose to be up-front with her daughter and approach the issue directly. She might say, "Sue, I realize that when you were young, I rescued you and did things for you that most other kids were doing for themselves. Now I realize I'm still rescuing you. I'm caring for your kids instead of letting you take responsibility for them. I don't want to rescue you anymore. What do you think we can do about that?"

Once the issue is in the open, Linda can negotiate with Sue using choices and enforceable limits. She can state what she is willing to do and let her daughter make choices within those parameters. If conditions for Linda become intolerable, she may need to make further decisions about her role in her grandchildren's lives. Those kinds of decisions are covered more fully in Chapter 9.

Understanding the Boundaries

Parents play a crucial role in your relationship with your grandchildren. Getting along and coming to agreement are crucial. Grandparents who don't can find themselves cut off from grandchildren, or find that time spent with them is more limited. This can be especially true in a case of divorce, where cooperation with in-laws is essential to spending time with grandkids.

Parents may not approve of grandparents' choices. As we mentioned earlier, a recent survey indicated that the primary problem parents have had with grandparental behavior is interference. The second most prevalent problem is overindulgence. Let's take a look at them both.

INTERFERENCE

There can be a bit of a double bind here for grandparents. Their support is desired, but not their interference. How do we know if we're overstepping the line?

🍎 *Interference is the opposite of giving the support a parent feels is needed.*

Interference steps over the boundary of support and makes behavior, intended to be helpful, offensive instead. Often parents don't feel they've been heard; they don't think grandparents have listened to them.

Grandparents' actions can legitimately be considered interference when they:

1. Criticize parents in front of children.
2. Provide unasked-for advice.
3. Undermine parental house rules.
4. Lower behavioral expectations of the grandchildren.

Grandparents who worry about interfering can ask their adult children for a signal when they've stepped over the line. "If I get out of line, ask me to find you a tissue. I will know I've gone too far and I'll head out to find one!"

OVERINDULGENCE

Many grandparents are so much more relaxed with their grandchildren than parents are that they enjoy them more, and are more tuned in to them as people. They are often less concerned with achievements than are the parents. Grandparents can be a natural emotional haven for grandchildren. Under these circumstances, it's not unusual for parents to perceive grandparents as indulgent.

Whether they are or not, grandparents need to be alert to this parental concern. Sometimes grandparents are more affluent than parents and can provide grandchildren what parents cannot. That provision is okay, as long as parents approve. When parents object, it's time to back off.

Sometimes parents will object to the number of sweets and candies available from Grandpa and Grandma. Grandparents can be tempted to break parents' rules regarding snacks. Being sneaky, however, is not a wise choice. Grandparents are wiser to be overt than covert. They need to discuss the issue with parents. "I really like giving the kids sweets, and I know how you feel about candy. Can we compromise on this in some way?" They may arrive at a compromise that limits the amount of candy, or substitutes sugarless candy or fruit.

❦ *The key is to listen to parents' thoughts and work to compromise.*

Being sneaky never works, because invariably grandchildren will spill the beans. They'll go back home and say, "At Grandma's house we get candy." If you ask them to keep it a secret, they will probably also announce,

"And Grandma told me not to tell you!"

The same open discussions about appropriateness may be needed if you sense parental discomfort with your gift-giving. Being honest and up-front can rescue a relationship from long-term nagging irritations, and will ensure your never having to keep anything secret.

WHEN PARENTS OBJECT TO LOVE AND LOGIC

Betsy, a grandmother with lots of energy, became so excited about Love and Logic principles when she learned about them that she studied them extensively and became one of our Love and Logic consultants. She was enthusiastic, and she let her son and daughter know. Every time she saw them, she preached the values of the Love and Logic approach.

One day, when caring for her granddaughter Vicky, she lost it, and shouted at her at the top of her voice. Her daughter, just returning to pick up Vicky, overheard her. "I'm so glad I got to see Love and Logic in action!" she teased. "I guess I'll have to try it sometime after all."

She never did, though. Betsy had gone overboard in her excitement about Love and Logic parenting. She could have prevented her daughter's negative response by a less fanatical approach. The best way to create enthusiasm for Love and Logic parenting is not by shoving a book at parents and saying, "This is wonderful—read it. It will change your life."

❦ *The way to create enthusiasm about a way of life is simply to model the approach. Instead of raving about Love and Logic grandparents, just be one.*

Parents will not object to modeling, but they will readily object to preaching. None of us likes to be told what to do and how to do it. As a matter of fact, a little mystery creates intrigue. When parents ask about it, be reticent, "Oh, it's something I've been experimenting with from a book I read. I'll share it with you sometime if you like."

When they ask again, share a copy of our book, *Parenting with Love and Logic,* and let them reach their own conclusions. Or casually mention one of our tapes. "I heard a good tape the other day. Let me know if you want a few good laughs sometime. I'll share it with you."

A sense of humor has smoothed many a rough spot in parent-child relationships!

≈ 7 ≈

When Your Grandchild's Parents Divorce

Learning is discovering
that something is possible.
—Fritz Perls

When divorce ends a marriage, a boulder crashes into the family pond and the ripples are felt by everyone. All three generations grieve lost relationships. Grandparents hurt for their children and their grandchildren, as well as for themselves. They ask, "What can I say? What can I do"—especially, "What can I do to help my grandchildren survive the waves without drowning?"

All relationships suddenly seem to be on shaky ground: How will this affect how I relate to my grandchildren? Will I still get to see them? How do I deal with my son and daughter-in-law? Do I get involved? Do I take sides? Grandparents' hearts and minds are filled with these questions while they themselves are grieving their loss and feeling as if they are sinking below the waterline.

There are no easy solutions to crashing boulders, and no way to prevent the surrounding waves from spreading around them. But there are a few flotation devices that may help prevent drowning.

Remember earlier we said that there are times when a grandparent can be a strong stabilizing force, especially for grandchildren? When your family's world goes topsy-turvy in the wake of divorce, this is one of those times.

Helping Grandchildren Deal with Feelings

When parents divorce, children are caught in a whirlpool of feelings. They may be numb, hurt, and, eventually, angry. Children often feel they are the cause of a split. They may be desperate to bring their parents back together. They may be absolutely certain their parents no longer love them.

Facing this powerful vortex of feelings, grandparents wonder, "What do I say? What do I do?"

There are no absolute answers to these questions. There are no words to take away the pain. There are no magic phrases that close the wound. There is no trick that can turn back the clock.

❧ *To ask, "What do I say?" is to ask the wrong question. Far more important questions are:*

"What do I ask?"
"How do I listen?"

Asking questions and listening are crucial to assuring children a way to express their feelings instead of suppressing them.

Tony, the Boiling Teakettle

A grandmother approached me (Jim) a few years ago after a presentation and asked for advice about her fifth-grade grandson. He had been a model student until this year, and now he was breaking every rule he could. I asked about his family.

"His parents went through a bitter divorce, but that was three years ago," she said. "Tony handled it very well. It didn't seem to affect him. In fact, he handled it far better than his parents did."

Tony was a boiling teakettle. He had plugged up his emotional spout in second grade, when he needed someone to listen. At that time, there was no one there to help him let the steam escape.
Over the years, the pressure had become intolerable. The steam had to come out sometime, somewhere, and in his fifth-grade class he found his pressure outlet.

Helping unplug the spout can be done with a gentle question, such as:

❖ "How are you handling this?"
❖ "How are you feeling about all of this?"
❖ "How are you doing?"

Questions can sometimes be statements followed by a pause:

❖ "This must be hard for you."
❖ "You must feel like you're in a thunderstorm right now."
❖ "I'm wondering how you explain all of this to yourself."

How a grandchild responds to these openers will determine where the conversation goes. As he or she responds, grandparents can follow the three basic principles for communication that we talked about earlier:

1. Listen
2. Give feedback to check for understanding
3. Respond

🍎 *In times of crisis, adults and children need to feel understood. They desperately want listening, not advice. They want understanding, not reassurance.*

If we leap in with reassurance and advice without first listening—listening well and listening hard—grandchildren will conclude, "They don't understand," or "They don't really care." There is no doubt about it. Kids survive the divorce of their parents better if they have an understanding adult to listen to them.

Justin's Message of Love

When Justin's parents divorced and his mother returned to work, his grandmother offered to care for him after school every day. One day, over peanut butter cookies and lemonade, grandma asked, "Justin, I've been wondering if you're doing okay. How are you feeling about what's been happening with your parents?"

For a few seconds the only sound was the crunching of peanut butter cookies. Then Justin said, "I don't know—I feel sort of dead inside sometimes. And I get so angry I want to hit someone. Why couldn't they stay married, Grandma?"

Grandma said softly, "I don't know, Justin, I don't know. I wish they could have stayed married too."

Silence again.

Then Justin said, "I miss Daddy."

"I know you do. It's sort of like there's this empty hole in your life, huh? When will he visit again?"

As Justin and Grandma talked, Grandma was actually sending him a very important message, one that she was telling him without words: "I love you. I am interested in you, and I want to hear about your feelings." That message, unstated, is more powerful than any words a grandparent could invent to try to take away the pain.

🐞 *Communicating the message of love and caring that lies beneath words actually expressed should be the primary concern in a grandparent's mind.*

Kids may need to air several issues when talking with an adult: issues about the past, about the future, and whether their parents still love them. Your grandchildren may also feel they are the only children who have ever experienced this pain. This is an opportune time for a grandparent to let them know they are not alone.

THE PAST

Most children whose parents divorce experience some self-blame. For some children this self-blame is stronger than for others. A child may think, "If I had been a better kid, my parents would not have gotten divorced."

When a grandchild raises this issue and has had time to air his feelings about it, a grandparent can clarify whether the child heard his parents fighting about him, or only thinks they may have fought about him. A grandparent can ask, "Would you like to hear what I think about that?"

If the grandchild agrees, the grandparent can say, "Parents fight about all sorts of things—even parents who don't get divorced. They fight about money, cars, houses, about how they spend their time, what to eat, who does what work, and, yes, about their kids, too, sometimes. But it's not the fault of their money that they get divorced. It's not the fault of the house, the food, or you. It's how they see things and what they believe they need from each other."

You may want to ask for feedback to see if your grandchild understands the concept. This is often accomplished through sentence completion. Start the sentence, stop in the middle without dropping your voice, and allow your grandchild to fill in the blank.

"So, since it's really not your fault, it's the fault of . . . "

THE FUTURE

When children of divorce look ahead, sometimes they see a black hole—just emptiness and darkness. Grandparents can help them create a light, after listening to their pain, by asking a simple question: "As you look ahead, do you think down the road you're going to survive this or not survive?"

Most often, after thinking it over, a kid will say, "You know, I think I'll survive." When he makes that statement, it becomes his reality. It is much more effective than if Grandpa says, "I know you'll survive." At that point it is only Grandpa's reality.

REASSURANCE OF LOVE

One grandchild whose parents had recently divorced asked her grandfather, "Grandpa, will you ever stop loving me?"

"Of course not, sweetheart," he said. "Whatever made you think that?"

"Daddy and Mommy stopped loving each other," she said.

Reassurance of your love may be helpful to your grandchild, even if he or she doesn't ask for it. "You know, of course, that my love for you cannot be changed by a divorce paper. I will always love you, no matter what."

A child may also need reassurance that his parents still love him or her. Reassurance of parental love can take this form: "Your parents are divorcing *each other* and that's sad. But that doesn't mean they are divorcing you. Each of your parents still loves you as much as they always did."

These comments are appropriate when both parents remain committed to their child. If a mother or father has deserted his or her role as a parent, reassurance of love is not appropriate. Perhaps sadness and reassurance of worth are the best comfort a grandparent can provide. A grandparent can say, "I don't know why your daddy left either, and it makes me really sad. I think you're a very special person, and I'm going to keep loving you forever and ever."

If you find it necessary to address the issue of the parent's desertion of his or her child, it is wise to treat it as a parent's problem. A grandparent can say, for example, "Your mother has trouble dealing with close relationships. Some people just do. She had trouble showing love even when she was a little girl. You are very lucky that those of us still around you—your dad, your grandpa, and I—love you very much."

REASSURANCE FOR KIDS WHO FEEL TOTALLY ALONE

For kids who feel alone—that they are the only children in the world experiencing this catastrophe—some reassurance to the contrary can help.

❦ *"Did you know you're not the only kid whose parents are divorcing? Every day in this country, one hundred kids have parents who get divorced."*

Odds are your grandchild will look at you wide-eyed and say, "Really?" You can follow this with more reassurance: "Yep. And most of them come out of it just fine. It hurts heaps, but they come out of it okay."

For a child who feels in danger of sinking beneath the waves, these words of survival can be a rescue ship on the horizon.

Talking with Kids About Their Parents

When discussing parents' behavior, it is in the best interest of your grandchild to follow two policies:

1. Avoid criticism of your grandchild's parents. We've mentioned this before, and we mention it again because it's really important to remember. It's okay to express your feelings of sadness, and your grief. You can listen to your grandchild express anger with a parent. But criticizing your grandchild's parent in his or her presence creates even more conflict inside that child. Here are two examples of what one man said to his grandchild. You can decide for yourself which works best.

Negative: "Your dad just can't hold a job. He's never been very responsible, and I'm sorry that it's hurting you."
Positive: "Your dad is going through a hard time right now. I'm sorry that his hard time is hurting you, too."

Instead of helping to stabilize his grandchild's world, the negative statement simply adds to the child's turbulence. The negative statement causes the grandchild to deal with not only his parents' divorce, but with newly discovered weaknesses in his role model.

The positive statement asks the child to recognize that his parent is having a rough time too and stirs up empathy rather than criticism. The child will feel more attention from a positive statement than he will from a statement focusing on someone else's mistakes.

2. Don't take sides. It is in the best interest of a child, if at all within the realm of possibility, to maintain a working relationship with both parents. When you take sides, even without saying a word, you are placing blame on one of them.

Negative: "Your mom did the right thing leaving your dad."
Positive: "Even though Dad had to leave, you and Mom will be okay."

Negative: "Dad simply was not treating Mom right."
Positive: "Sometimes people don't treat each other the way they need to be treated. You and I treat each other great, though, don't we?"

❖ ❖ ❖

Negative: "Dad's got a lot to learn."
Positive: "I know you hurt, but everybody can learn something from times like these. Sometimes you don't know what you've learned until later."

The only time when taking sides is viable is when you see it as necessary—for instance, when one parent has been abusive and laws are being violated. Otherwise, you don't want to encourage your grandchild to fuel an already scorching fire.

Handling Misbehavior Problems

In the turmoil of feelings that follow parental divorce, children can develop behavior problems. Some become aggressive and disobedient, refusing to follow rules at home or at school. Others regress to earlier undesirable behaviors, or try shoplifting. A child may try taking a prized possession of yours, using *things* to provide comfort in a time of great insecurity. Under any stress, kids are likely to regress to more immature modes of behavior.

One temptation for parents and grandparents is to tolerate misbehavior because of the emotional turmoil. But this is not a wise choice.

❦ *Just because the emotional roots of a child's behavior are understood doesn't mean the behavior itself is acceptable.*

You can't simply say to yourself, "I know she is acting that way because of the divorce." Unacceptable behavior is still unacceptable. Extra leeway is not helpful to a child suffering through parental divorce. Giving a grandchild some emotional outlet by *listening* may minimize negative behavior, but any negative behavior must be responded to immediately.

The guidelines for behavior during a time of divorce are:

1. Acknowledge the feeling. It's okay to talk about hurt feelings. "I'm sorry Mom left." "My chest hurts when I think about Dad." "I know this is rough for you." "Do you want to talk about how you're feeling?" "I'm worried about you. Are you okay?"

2. Maintain the same behavior standards. "Everyone around here knows this is a hard time. This is not, however, an excuse to lower our standards of behavior. Even in difficult times, we play by the same rules."

Grandparents can send the message, "When the going gets tough, the tough get going." The underlying principle is that understanding the causes of negative behavior is good, but understanding it does not make that behavior acceptable.

Parents undergoing divorce may feel guilty, depressed, and overwhelmed. Confronted with negative behavior, they may think, "I'm having trouble coping. Melissa is also having trouble, and I'm partly to blame." Because they blame themselves, they may hesitate to enforce their usual behavior standards.

❦ *Grandparents can encourage parents to not let down their standards—but only with permission.*

Sometimes, negative behavior can provide a springboard for asking about a child's feelings. If a grandchild is sulking or going around slamming doors or disobeying, wait for a calm moment and ask if his behavior has anything to do with you. After all, tell him, if you are a cause, you'd like to know. If he says no, you can assume a counselor role: "Is there a different reason that you'd like to talk about?" If he says no, simply thank him for being honest. If yes, you have opened a door to his being able to vent his feelings in a more acceptable way.

Often when parents and grandparents are hurting and overwhelmed, they fail to notice a child who has become depressed or withdrawn and fail to see the need for dealing with the child's grief.

It's important for a grandparent, who may be more objective during divorce proceedings, to be alert enough to notice a withdrawn or depressed child and call this to the attention of the child's parent.

Grandparents and Visitation Rights

To take sides against a parent who has custody of your grandchildren is risky and unwise. Not only do you add to your grandchildren's mental burden, but you weaken the connection that allows you to continue to see them. Few states have laws that require that grandparents be allowed visitation rights, although most states now have some laws addressing grandparents' rights. If you need to know what those laws are, check with your local bar association or a local lawyer.

You may want to communicate a positive, caring message to the custodial parent early on in the divorce process. An example might be, "I hope we can continue to interact with the children. We think it would be a good thing—for us, for the kids, and for you. Here's why."

It could help to be up front about your emotional support and about not taking sides: "We don't want in any way to make things more difficult for you. If we accidentally do, please tell us."

Trying to maintain visitation rights by demanding them, in true drill-sergeant fashion, or by wringing your hands and begging your adult children to not do this to you, is to court rebellion and be denied the very thing you want most. Since you have no legal ground to stand on, the only thing you succeed in doing is in making yourself look foolish.

If the worst-case scenario happens and you lose contact with your grandchildren following divorce, it may be comforting to take a long view of things the way Roy and Melody did.

Roy and Melody's Good News

Roy and Melody spent a lot of time with their grandchildren until the kids were seven and nine. Then their mother took them with her when she left her husband for another man. Roy said, "We knew we had lost contact with the grandchildren. The bad news is that Janice is a poor parent and will probably blow it with them. The good news is that a year or more from now they'll remember their good times with us and we feel certain one way or another they will contact us. In the meantime, we must content ourselves with the fact that we gave them a lot during those early years, and we feel that what we gave them will stick, even though we won't see them for some time."

Another set of grandparents who lost visitation rights are counting the days until their grandson is eighteen. That's when he'll be able to take charge of his own life and when they'll be able to renew their relationship. What gets them through this long wait is understanding and accepting that this is their only alternative and that their relationship with their grandson, based on strong early bonding, is only going to get better.

When Children and Grandchildren Move Back Home

In the wake of divorce, when a son or daughter wants to move back home with your grandchild, your life as you know it is up for some hard changes. That's why it's essential to establish a clear understanding of the ground rules up front.

🍎 *The more deep-seated the problems that caused the adult child and his or her children to move back home, the more important it is to have a written contract between you.*

By seeking an up front agreement, you demonstrate the Love and Logic principle of taking care of yourself. You model adult behavior for both your adult child and your grandchildren. Some of the issues to be agreed upon, preferably *before* parent and grandchild begin living with you, are:

❖ *House rules:* Will boyfriends or girlfriends be allowed to stay overnight? Will smoking and drinking alcohol be permitted? What about parties?

❖ *Financial support:* Who pays for what?
❖ *Child care:* How much baby-sitting are grandparents expected to provide?
❖ *Division of labor:* Who is responsible for which household tasks?
❖ *Quiet times:* How late will the stereo be played?
❖ *The role of parent:* Will grandparents resume some parenting responsibilities?
❖ *Discipline:* Who will take primary responsibility for disciplining grandchildren and enforcing house rules?
❖ *Length of stay:* How long is the term of this live-in status? And how do we go about informing one another if the live-in arrangement is not working out?

One set of grandparents and a parent we know agreed that when all reasonable attempts to work out a problem or dispute had failed, a red bow would be tied on the refrigerator door, which would be considered a two-week notice for moving out.

🍒 *No matter what the situation, it is important for everyone to understand that the three-generation arrangement is not forever.*

Written agreements are not hard-hearted or cold. They are simply a way of making life run more smoothly and taking care of yourself as well. They encourage the parties involved to think ahead and understand their roles in the relationship. We know one set of grandparents who rented a storage unit for their son's things until the details of the agreement were worked out. They sat down with him and discussed all their issues when he announced that he wanted to move in. When he learned about their no-smoking policy, and no-overnight-girlfriends policy, he opted to live elsewhere.

Stabilizing the Ship

People going through divorce are people awash in change. Sometimes they are in crisis and we say to them, "If you need me, let me know." But people in crisis may be depressed, or not thinking clearly. They may not have the clarity of mind to know what they need from you, or may not have the energy to ask for it.

Sometimes it's helpful to offer to your adult children assistance in a more concrete form. Some examples are:

"Christy, would you like me to do the shopping for you to save you some time?"

"John, would you like me to have the kids over on Saturday morning, so you can have some time to yourself?"

❦ *When you offer your time or energy, only offer if you can make an offer that's concrete and specifically geared to meet the needs of the moment.*

Divorce, whenever it occurs, can send disturbing waves through the family system. By handling it wisely, we can help prevent the family from capsizing. No journey is without incident, but yours can be smoother if you keep the following in mind:

❖ Grandparents can be a stabilizing force for grandchildren when their world goes topsy-turvy in the wake of divorce. Help a child see it's not his or her fault that parents are divorcing.

❖ Kids survive their parents' divorce better when they have an understanding, objective adult to listen to them. Instead of "What do I say?" remember to ask yourself, "What do I ask?" and "How do I listen?"

❖ Every chance you get, let your grandchild know in some way, "I love you. I am interested in you. I want to hear your feelings." Reassure your grandchildren that you will always love them, no matter what.

❖ Instead of telling kids, "I know you'll survive this," ask them, "You think you're going to survive this down the road?" Give them room to speak *their* reality, not yours.

❖ Ask kids, "Did you know that every day in this country, 100 kids have parents who get divorced—that you're not the only one going through this?"

❖ Don't criticize your grandchild's parent, and don't take sides. Maintain your best possible working relationship with both parents. This helps your grandchild's mental state and can help your visitation rights.

❖ Remember that just because emotional roots of behavior are understood doesn't mean the behavior itself is acceptable. Help kids understand that a divorce in the family is not an excuse to misbehave.

❖ Offer to help a parent in divorce only when you can offer concrete assistance, like shopping or taking the kids for an afternoon.

❖ When an adult child with children wants to return home to live with you, put together a written agreement. Settle issues of potential difference before they move in.

❖ Divorce is a difficult time for all three generations. Be concerned about everyone's welfare, without forgetting about your own.

When Your Family Includes Step-grandchildren

*We are not permitted to choose
the frame of our destiny. But what
we put into it is ours.*
—Dag Hammarskjöld

Keith and Lillian Meet Jason

Keith and Lillian's daughter Rachel, who lived just across town from them, remarried when her son Daniel was four. Her remarriage brought into the family circle a five-year-old stepson, Jason. Keith and Lillian were happy with their daughter's remarriage and appreciated her new husband.

Jason was about to join Rachel and her family this summer, and Keith and Lillian were uncertain how to handle the change. They were uneasy because they didn't feel the same affection for Jason as they did for Daniel. They wondered about how to treat the two boys. Should they invite Jason to play each time they invite Daniel? Should Jason call them Grandpa and Grandma as Daniel does? Should they give both boys the same kind of birthday presents?

When remarriage occurs a whole family system changes. Everyone makes adjustments. There are new people to meet and incorporate into the family circle, new personalities, and new likes and dislikes to accommodate. There are differing histories of parenting techniques and family rituals and traditions to change or adjust to. There is also an air of uncertainty and a measure of fear.

Don and Sherry Get Two New Granddaughters

Don and Sherry were concerned about the upcoming holidays. Their son had recently remarried the mother of two teenage daughters. They had met the girls only twice, and one of those times was at the wedding. They didn't know what to expect for the holidays and were concerned about whether the girls would be comfortable and wondered whether there would be behavior problems with either of them. They had seen the older girl smoking and didn't know how to tell her that due to Don's allergies, smoking was not permitted in their home.

Caught in the Middle

The dominant sensation for everyone involved in a stepfamily is that of being caught in the middle. The stepparent feels caught between new spouse and children. The parent feels caught between spouse and biological children. The children feel caught between parents.

Often a new stepfather feels that his wife lets her biological children get away with too much. He is sometimes uncomfortable with the level of back-talk and what he sees as evasion of responsibilities. A new stepmother may often feel that her husband gives his biological children too much, such as money for toys, cars, and college. Neither of them is sure of his or her right to discipline the stepchildren. Should she step in or let him handle that? Should he leave those issue up to her or discipline now, when they need it?

Grandparents feel caught in the middle, too—between their son or daughter and the new son or daughter-in-law, and sometimes even the ex-spouse. They can also feel caught between the two generations—parent and child, and parent and stepchild.

Children, already uncertain in this period of transition, sense insecurity among the adults in their lives. In their helplessness, in order to gain some sense of power, they may try to play the adults off against each other, taking on an attitude of "divide and conquer." When a child of divorce succeeds in being divisive, however, *everyone* loses.

❦ *The best service grandparents can provide for parents is support and affirmation in the presence of their children.*

Backing parental policy and expecting parental backing of your own house rules are important in any family. They are crucial in blended families that have the burden of added stress. Grandparents may wish to sit down with a son or daughter and say, "I don't want to get in the middle of things with you and your new family and cause any problems. Please tell me how I can best support you at this time."

Don and Sherry Reveal House Rules

Don and Sherry would be wise to make a long distance phone call a few weeks before Christmas to discuss the smoking issue with their son and new daughter-in-law, to be sure they are in agreement about the issue. They can express their interest in the girls' welfare as well: "We'd really like the girls to have a nice time here, and we'd like to know if there is anything we ought to know. What about food likes and dislikes? Are they on diets? Are they outdoor or indoor people? Are there any behavior issues we should know about?"

For all practical purposes, the first time these stepdaughters visit, Sherry and Don are taking two strangers into their home, and they have a strong need for information. They must ask for the information they need, and their adult children must be willing to provide that information. When prepared, Sherry and Don can do their part to make the Christmas visit as pleasant as possible.

John and Ann's Christmas

John and Ann had a slightly different Christmas vacation experience. John said, "I know the whole situation was difficult for Carl because he had to deal with Susan and her spoiled, bratty kid. He worried about what we would think of them. There was so much uncertainty in the air the first few days of their visit, you could have cut it with a knife. On the third day we sat both Carl and Susan down and said, 'Look, we know the two of you may have some disagreements on how to handle the kids, and we don't want to get in the middle of that. We simply would like to explain our house rules.' After we explained our expectations for mealtimes, putting things away, and caring for our home, things went a whole lot smoother."

❦ *Grandparents have a right to expect their house rules to be followed—no matter whether kids present are children, grandchildren, or step-grandchildren.*

Developing Affection for Step-Grandchildren

Because step-grandchildren come to a family system as outsiders and strangers, it is natural for grandparents to not feel the affection for them they feel for their biological grandchildren—some with whom they've built bonds for decades. To expect instant intimacy is asking for something beyond anyone's reach. Feeling the pressure to create intimacy quickly, some grandparents overdo. To pretend instant intimacy is to invite distrust. The step-grandparent who tells a child, "You are part of our family now and we love you just as much as our other grandchildren," risks suspicion on the part of the new children. Children recognize ambivalence or a con job when they hear one.

❦ *It is better for a step-grandparent to open a door to intimacy rather than pretend it.*

Lillian Levels with Jason

In a quiet moment with her step-grandson, Lillian told him, "Jason, you know Daniel has been in our family a long time and we know him very well and love him very much. We're glad to have a chance now to get to know you too. It takes time to love people, and we hope that, as we get to know each other, we will all come to love each other just as much."

Reaffirming Affection for Grandchildren

When stepchildren enter a family system, a biological grandchild may need reassurance too. He or she may feel that the "new kid on the block" is stealing attention.

Daniel Takes Cues

Daniel is a case in point. When Jason came on the scene as a step-grandchild, Daniel felt his "number-one-attraction" status in the family was threatened. He acted out this fear by testing limits. He took down his grandfather's pool table equipment without permission.

Grandpa Keith told him, "Daniel, I will continue to love you no matter what. Nothing you do can make me love you any less. I'm unhappy, though, about your taking out the pool cues. Even though I love you, I cannot accept this behavior—which, by the way, is unlike you. What's going on?"

Recent studies show that the age at which stepchildren enter a family system affects the nature of the bond between grandparents and step-grandchildren.

❦ *Step-grandchildren who enter a family system at ten years of age or younger tend to form stronger bonds than those who enter at adolescence.*

This information can be helpful to you if a new

step-grandchild over the age of ten has entered your life. This may be a child who can benefit from warm, caring grandparenting even more than you imagined.

Stopping Favoritism Before It Starts

In one of our Grandparent Focus Groups at the Love and Logic Institute, a grandparent said, "I have two wonderful grandsons, and I jut acquired three new step-granddaughters. They are adorable little girls, but I don't know whether I can love them the same over time as my grandsons."

One group member responded, "You'll love them in time, but your own grandchildren will come first."

Another group member added quickly, "Mask that feeling as much as possible, and reach out to them as much as you can."

🍎 *Although grandparents may feel differently about their grandchildren and step-grandchildren, they are wise to treat them the same.*

When you stand in step-grandchildren's shoes for a moment and look at the world from their point of view, you can more easily understand why they need to be treated with as much attention as your grandkids. It is not their fault that their parents divorced and remarried. All they can see is that their "brother" or "sister" is more loved, more esteemed, if he or she receives a better birthday present.

When Keith and Lillian bought a Pirate Ship Leggo set for Daniel for his birthday, they bought the same size Airplane Leggo set for Jason on his birthday. They had seen their friends make the mistake of buying a portable CD player for a grandson and giving a birthday card to a step-granddaughter when her birthday arrived. Four years later, the step-granddaughter was still bitter.

When Feelings Do Not Follow

Although they have given themselves and their step-grandchild time and energy to begin to build a bond, occasionally grandparents may find themselves still alienated from, and unable to accept, a step-grandchild. It's important in this case to determine whether the alienation has an internal or external cause.

Do other people groan and head the other way when the child enters the living room door? In such a case, the grandparent's reaction is justified, and perhaps adults in the child's life need to pool their energies and establish a plan to help the child reshape his or her responses to the world.

Do others find that child likeable? Are they able to establish a relationship with him or her? If so, and the grandparent is alone in his or her feelings, a different plan of action is in order. Perhaps it is the grandparent who needs to do some self-exploration to uncover the causes of his or her alienation. Discomfort understood, he or she may wish to acknowledge the issue with the step-grandchild and be open about it.

One grandfather told his step-grandson, "I'm sorry, Sam. It's not your fault, but I have trouble dealing with shoulder-length hair and earrings on guys. I know that other people have no problem with it, but I do. It's an issue I need to learn to deal with, and I just want you to know that I realize it's my problem and not yours."

By acknowledging his difficulty, Sam's step-granddad caught a virus in the bud. He realized that he himself was the one spreading the disease of misunderstanding. By openly letting Sam know about his realization and how he honestly felt, he began to build the one thing both of them truly wanted: a bond.

When You're Thinking About Raising Your Grandchild

Things do not change—we do
—Henry David Thoreau

According to the United States Census Bureau, more than three million children in the United States now live with their grandparents, a dramatic increase in just a few years. More than a million of these children live with their grandparents without either parent present. In all, about 5 percent of American families consist of grandparents raising one or more grandchildren.

These statistics include only children living with grandparents. If you add the number of grandparents providing full-time day care, the number of grandchildren being raised by grandparents rises even higher.

The reason children live with their grandparents is often one of the four D's: death, divorce, desertion, or drug abuse. But there are other reasons as well, such as a parent's (primarily mother's) emotional difficulties.[14]

When grandparents make the choice to raise a grandchild, the word "grand" easily fades, because in these situations, grandparents become parents.

Two Considerations and Three Questions

For some grandparents, living with grandchildren may be a bit like travelling with friends. At first, a sleeping bag under the pines and a campfire are very exciting. But after a week, a box spring and an electric range begin to look very attractive.

When you choose to raise a grandchild, the arrangement isn't as easy to end as a camping trip. It's a long-term, life-changing decision. Two factors are vital.

1. The decision must be a conscious one rather than a situation that simply evolves.

The raising of a grandchild may often begin with no real decision at all. It can start as a temporary situation or one that happens sporadically, sparked by as simple a question as, "Can you take Cindy for a few days while we get our heads together?" and end as day care that lasts years or decades.

2. Grandparents are advised to get professional help from a psychiatrist or psychologist and from a lawyer.

The decision to raise a grandchild is so complex and so loaded with emotional traps that professional help is crucial in sorting through feelings and reasons for taking on and not taking on such a mammoth responsibility. Legal counsel can help sort through the complexities of guardianship and custody—temporary or permanent, legal or physical.

Grandparents who have helicopter tendencies are likely to gather all their aerodynamic forces and hover the moment they uncover a need to parent a second time around. If they don't rush in and try to fix the problem, they may feel guilty. Their grandchildren need a home, and it seems there is no other place but theirs. What other choice do they have? If they don't raise their grandchildren, who else possibly could?

Solving a problem to keep from feeling guilty, however, is not sufficient reason. Although solving a problem for someone may be a form of love, sometimes *not* solving that problem can be a higher form of love. If rescuing your adult child is your motivation, you need to think twice before acting. Should you continue to rescue your child? Could he or she benefit in the long run from your not taking on your grandchild?

Before consulting any professional for outside help, there are three soul-searching questions to ask yourself and answer as honestly as you can:

1. Am I able to raise this grandchild?

Being "able" means having the personal financial resources or access to available financial support from the child's parents or from funds available to the child from Social Services. Being able also means having the health, energy, and emotional strength to care for the child *until he or she becomes an adult.*

2. Am I willing to raise this grandchild?

Being able is one thing. Are you willing to make the commitment to raise your grandchild? Are you willing to reenter the joys and trials of parenting a second time around? Are you willing to give the energy, time, and emotional commitment required? What would you be giving up by taking on this task? Does the child have special needs, such as developmental delays or behavior problems as a result of the parents' treatment of him or her? If so, are you willing to take on the *added* financial responsibility and time commitment required to care for this child?

3. Do I want to raise this grandchild?

Being willing and able are important. But digging deeper still, do you *want* to take on this responsibility? Can you do it without feeling trapped, without feeling as if you had no choice in the matter? It is not a favor to a child to be raised by someone who had no choice. If you suspect that you are going to resent raising this child, perhaps there are others who would be better choices as parents.

What's to Gain and What's to Lose

The only time a roller coaster is fun is when you are *expecting* a roller coaster ride. When you are settled in for a leisurely journey, a roller coaster ride can turn your trip into disaster. Some peoples' experiences parenting their grandchildren are just that.

In an in-depth study of 114 grandparents, Margaret Jendrek found significant gains and losses for grandparents raising grandchildren.[15]

THE LOSSES

◆ Time for fun and recreation
◆ Money
◆ Contact with friends, relatives, and neighbors
◆ Enjoyment of daily activities
◆ Privacy
◆ Belief that grandparenting is fun
◆ Time for self
◆ Enough time to get everything done
◆ Time for, and giving attention to, spouse
◆ Satisfaction with relationship with spouse

Those who felt these losses also reported increases in:

Worry
Edgy or upset feelings
Feeling emotionally drained

THE GAINS

◆ Contact with neighbors
◆ A renewed purpose for living
◆ More common goals to share with spouse

Barbara and Stuart had lived at their new location for two years with just a nodding acquaintance with their next-door neighbors. When their grandchildren came to live with them and started playing with the kids next door, Barbara and the neighbors' kids' mother became friends also. "She's added a new dimension to my life," said Barbara. "I like having a friend from a younger generation. It keeps me young."

"Having Danny has brought my husband and me closer," said Lynn. "We'd each been pursuing our own interests—Bill golfed and I played bridge. Danny gives us something in common again. I'm grateful for that."

BETTER THE SECOND TIME AROUND

Some grandparents see parenting their grandchildren as a second chance—an opportunity to avoid making the mistakes they made the first time around. It's almost as if this might be a way to right their wrongs.

One grandfather remembered, "When my kids were growing up I believed that dads didn't hug. I remember when my daughter was 12 and she was riding with me in the front seat, she put her head on my shoulder and I knew she wanted me to put my arm around her. But I was a good dad; I didn't do that. Now I get sick when I think about it. I don't want to make the same mistakes with my grandchildren. I make sure there are plenty of hugs."

Some grandparents recognize that they were helicopters or drill sergeants when they were raising their own children, and want to be consultants this time around. Rather than rescue or issue orders, they want to allow their grandchildren to grow up to be responsible adults, allowing them to make lots of decisions while they are young and to learn life's lessons by living with the consequences of unwise choices.

If you are parenting the second time around, you may want to consider getting some parent training. Here are some reasons we think retraining can be helpful:

❖ You can avoid making the same mistakes you made with your children.

❖ You may have a mammoth parenting task ahead of you. A child burdened with stress and chaos takes better-than-average parenting to produce average results.

❖ Children today face issues your children never had to deal with, such as drugs, gangs, and violence.

For more information on parenting, please see our earlier books, *Parenting with Love and Logic* and *Parenting Teens with Love and Logic,* or contact Cline/Fay's Love and Logic Institute to inquire about audiotapes, videotapes and books available to you. The address and a toll-free number are listed at the back of this book.

LOVE AND LOGIC TIP 19
Four Steps to Responsibility

Over my years as a school principal, I (Jim) came to realize that creating responsible children is a four-step process:

1. *Give a child the chance to act responsibly.*
2. *Hope and pray the child makes a mistake.*
3. *When the child makes a mistake, stand back and allow consequences, accompanied by liberal doses of empathy.*
4. *Give the child exactly the same assignment, offering him or her another chance to act responsibly.*

You can use this process with any responsibility, no matter how small. You can, for example, let a child decide whether or not to wear her coat on a chilly day. You hope she decides to go without a coat. Then when she's walking with her teeth chattering, you empathize, "I'm sorry you're so cold." But you don't offer to give up your coat for her. You let her suffer the consequences. Five minutes in the cold air never did permanent damage.

The next day you give her exactly the same choice again. This second opportunity lets her know you think she's wise enough to learn from her mistakes.

Legal Considerations

Parents who give up custody of their children almost always have ambivalent feelings about it. Unless grandparents share a clear understanding with parents, they could be asking for a roller coaster ride of staggering proportions. Parents often change their minds, lengthen the stay, shorten it, or want the children back after permanently giving them up. You need to reach an agreement.

❦ *Get your agreement in writing.*
An ounce of prevention is worth a ton of cure.

Educate yourself about legal statuses and what they can mean. Keep in mind that definitions and options vary by state. That's why we recommend that you contact qualified legal counsel. Many grandparents don't want to have to deal with attorneys on this matter, but we are long-time members of the "ounce of prevention" school. Seek legal standing as soon as possible, whether guardianship or legal custody.

❖ *Physical custody (guardianship):* This right guarantees physical possession of the child. In other words, the right to have a child live with you and the responsibility of providing daily care.
❖ *Legal custody:* The right to make decisions pertaining to the child's upbringing. This authority can include decisions regarding education, medical care, and discipline.

Grandparents report that when their children have consented to their taking legal custody, the transition has gone smoothly. When parents have contested the case, the situation has been agonizing. Verbal, then written, agreement is essential.

When you take physical custodianship, it is important to ask: How long will this child be with us? Is there a definite end to this? What is the timetable? Under what conditions will you wish her back? What are the conditions of return? Adoption is the only status that's permanent.

There is a variety of conditions under which grandparent "parents" have grandchildren living with them. Some are caring for them at the request of the parents; others are doing so at the request of the state. Some have temporary custody; others, permanent. A few have adopted their grandchildren.

Grandparents may simply be housing grandchildren without a legally defined relationship. In this situation, they are not authorized by law to make decisions about their grandchild, and they live each day with the possibility of the parent(s), fit or unfit, returning and reclaiming the child.

When it comes to children, possession is not nine-tenths of the law. Some grandparents have reported an unfit parent coming to their door, escorted by police, to reclaim a child. Unaware of their fourth amendment rights, grandparents have given the child to this parent. Unless parents have a warrant to search your house and seize your grandchild, you don't have to open your door. If there is no warrant, neither your child nor the police have a right to enter.

If you didn't know this until now, there's a chance that there are other legal ramifications you will want to learn before moving ahead.

❧ *When making a decision whether to raise your grandchild(ren), always consult legal counsel.*

When a Parent Wants a Child Back

What happens when a parent wants a child back? There is no simple answer to this question. Many factors enter into the wisdom and outcome of such a transition. Is the parent competent? How will the child adjust? Will his outlook or well-being be hampered by such a change? Is she happy where she is now? Can we trust the child's judgment in deciding the best place for him to live? Are parents—or the caretakers they provide for their child—abusive? Will positive values a child has learned fade by changing the child's home?

In many states, when children reach the age of 13, they have a legal voice in deciding where they live. When children are younger, their wishes are given varying weight. Statistically, the majority of children who live with their grandparents are very, very young. For these children, there are a number of major considerations.

First, age of grandparents. Perhaps no one can promise a child 20 years, but grandparents who are 60 or more may not be able to offer the resources and energy a young child requires to grow into a healthy adult. There may be court and custody battles. Will you have the drive to fight for the child's best interests? Will courts who see grandparents as too old, too frail, or too ill decide in your favor?

Will you decide to not buy medication you need because your grandchild needs a new pair of shoes? Will you unwittingly deny yourself attention you need in order to care for this new person in your life? Most grandparents will put themselves in jeopardy for the welfare of a grandchild, if necessary. If you do, is this the opposite of what you need to do for the long-term interest of that child?

Faced with returning a child to a dangerous home situation, asking him how he feels about it seems preposterous. Many children, afraid to speak out, are returned to parents who neglect and/or abuse them. Sometimes grandparents are aware of such a situation and can prove nothing and, therefore, do nothing to save the child. Grandparents are all too often painfully aware that their grandchildren are leaving the only home they've known that offers them safety and love.

If your grandchild is about to be returned to a biological parent, and you are concerned for his or her welfare, there are some steps you can take.[16] Teach your grandchild:

❖ Your area code and telephone number.
❖ How to adjust water temperatures in a bathtub, turning on the cold water and adding hot until the temperature is comfortable.
❖ To make sandwiches without using microwaves and ovens (until old enough to understand the safety required).
❖ How to hand-wash clothing in a sink.
❖ To talk with principal, teachers, or counselors if there are any problems, particularly if the child has been warned not to call you for fear of punishment from parents.

Trouble-Shooting and Support Resources

When a parent wants a child back, it may not always be in the best interest of the child to go with that parent.

It will be essential for you to do as much research as you possibly can to determine the fitness of your grandchild's future home. If you have any doubts regarding safety and comfort, get help immediately. You can get information and support by contacting ROCKING at (616) 683-9038, or by writing:

ROCKING/
Raising Our Children's Kids:
An Intergenerational Network of Grandparenting, Inc.
P. O. Box 96
Niles, Michigan 49120

We can't anticipate all the possible areas to troubleshoot when raising grandchildren, but we'd like to highlight a few we know can happen:

1. If you have worked consistently on a behavior problem for three months and made no progress, get help. Check with other grandparent "parents," teachers, counselors, psychologists, or your pediatrician. Don't wait for the problem to get worse.

2. When your grandchild's teacher, school counselor, or pediatrician expresses concern about his or her development—social or academic—pay close attention.

One of the biggest problems for grandparent "parents" is denial of a problem. When people have expertise in child development, at least try their skills.

3. Excessive interest in sex at a young age may be an indication of prior sexual abuse. Sexual activity is more overt today than it was a decade or two ago. Still, if you suspect prior sexual abuse, seek professional counseling for your grandchild.

Grandparent "parents" may find themselves in need of emotional support. They may discover that their bridge club members no longer appreciate the presence of a toddler. One grandmother, who decided to try a Mothers of Preschoolers (MOPS) group, gave this report:

Grandma Goes to MOPS

"I got there and found I was the oldest woman there by several decades. I was uncomfortable, because I was sure they were judging my parenting skills. After all, if my daughter had defaulted and I had my granddaughter, I must have been a bad parent, right? But I took a deep breath each week and pointed the car in the direction of the group. I knew I needed support.

At the third session, I realized those young moms didn't see me as someone who screwed up my daughter's life. They were looking to me as a senior advisor. It became an invigorating experience. Now I head there each week with no effort. I'm soaking it up!"

Because of the growing number of grandparents raising their grandchildren, the American Association of Retired Persons (AARP) has created a variety of resources for them. The organization offers information on research/statistics, financial, emotional, medical, and legal issues, as well as support groups. Resources include "Grandparents Raising Their Grandchildren: What to Consider and Where to Find Help," a brochure on visitation rights and how to obtain them, along with a listing of local grandparent support groups, and a quarterly newsletter. These materials and others may be obtained by calling (202) 434-2296 or by writing to:

AARP Grandparent Information Center
Social Outreach and Support
601 E Street, NW
Washington, DC 20049

Another organization that serves as a network and can offer help in setting up a support group or other program for grandparent "parents" in your area is:

National Coalition of Grandparents
137 Larkin Street
Madison, Wisconsin 53705
(608) 238-8751

THE BOTTOM LINE

Children generally handle things as well as the adults in their life do. If adults accept a situation, kids will accept it too. If adults wring their hands over it, kids will do the same. A heart-to-heart talk with a child, using active listening, can be one of your most helpful tools. Remember heart-to-hearts are almost always pure questions:

"This is really hard for me to talk about, but it's important. I need to know, how are you feeling about going back to your dad?"

"I'm really upset."

Remember that the key to active listening is to reflect what the child has just said and then explore it in more detail. For example:

"I can see you're upset. I understand that this is hard for you. What's the hardest thing about it for you?"

❦ *After a child has had time to explore and express feelings, an important message to give is that your love crosses all barriers.*

When grandparents have made the choice to raise their grandchildren—and have made it freely—and when they have taken the time to learn new parenting skills, most find that they are satisfied with their choice. Despite the demands, they find rewards. They say, given the same choice now, they would do it again.

One grandmother said, "Although I resent the circumstances that brought them here, I do not now resent, nor have I ever resented, these children. They are wonderful and precious to me." That, we believe, is the bottom line.

ᔕ10ᔓ

Becoming Grandparents
Too Soon

I think the necessity of being ready increases.
Look to it.
—Abraham Lincoln

I'm too young to be a grandparent!" That's often the
first thought of many men and women when they
learn their first grandchild is on the way. Becoming a
grandmother or grandfather is a new stage of life and it
requires an adjustment in thinking.

One grandmother announced that her grandchildren would be able to address her with any title they
liked—her first name, her last name, a made-up nickname—but there was one term she absolutely forbade
them to use: "Grandma!"

The rebellion against the grandparent stereotype
quadruples in impact when the grandchild-to-be is the
child of a pregnant teenager. Parents feel they have
entered a time warp in a world out of whack. In reality,
they could still be the parents of a new baby themselves.

This kind of thinking is normal and happens to all first-time grandparents-to-be—with the possible exception of those who've been hinting to their sons and daughters for years that it's time to have children.

New Situations Trigger Old Feelings

This feeling of not being ready—along with a violated standard of morality—can result in the return of helicopter and drill sergeant behavior, and asking questions such as, "How could you do this to me?"

When a teen becomes pregnant, statements like, "I'm not ready," and questions such as, "What have I done to deserve this?," are part of the helicopter personality's whirlwind of powerful emotions that surround an event such as this. One grandfather said, "I was so disappointed when I found out my daughter was pregnant—so angry—that I kept beating on the couch arm until it almost broke. I had to leave the house and go out for a walk."

A drill sergeant approach doesn't help either. Drill sergeants say, "I told you and told you not to experiment with sex, but you wouldn't listen. Now here's what you'll have to do . . . " When you order a son or daughter what decision to make, you can count on reprisal later. When your children experience guilt or pain about the decision—whatever the decision—the fall guy will be you. Instead of learning from the experience, they will transform their pain into anger—with you.

The consultant approach works best. As a consultant, you and your daughter and/or son can consider the following options together:

LOVE AND LOGIC TIP 20
Guiding Kids to Own and Solve Their Own Problems

When children have a problem, there are five steps adults can follow to help them own and solve that problem.

1. Show empathy.
2. Imply the child is smart enough to solve the problem.
3. Ask permission to share alternatives.
4. Look at the consequences of each alternative.
5. Let the child decide to solve or not to solve the problem.

When Ronnie told his grandpa that kids were picking on him and calling him names, Grandpa followed the five-step process in this way.

Grandpa empathized. "I bet you feel embarrassed."

Ronnie nodded. "Embarrassed and mad," he said.

"What do you think you're going to do about it?" asked Grandpa. Grandpa's question told Ronnie that Grandpa believed Ronnie could solve the problem. Ronnie's mind immediately went to work on solving the problem.

"I don't know," Ronnie said.

"Would you like to hear what some other kids have tried?" asked Grandpa.

"Yes." Ronnie gave him permission to share alternatives.

"Some kids go out and bust those name-callers in the mouth . . . some call them names . . . some tell them to stop, or get an adult to tell them . . . others send 'I-messages' about how it feels to be picked on and called names."

When Grandpa had listed possible solutions, he and Ronnie evaluated them. Ronnie said that the kids were bigger than he was and might hurt him if he tried to bust them in the mouth. He had already tried telling them to stop.

When they had finished evaluating the list, Ronnie still wasn't sure what he wanted to do.

"Well," Grandpa said. "I'm sure you'll make a wise choice. Good luck!" And they went out to play catch. Grandpa knew that even if Ronnie made a poor decision, Ronnie would still have a valuable learning experience.

- ❖ Keep the child and raise it
- ❖ Marry the other parent of the child
- ❖ Give the child up for adoption
- ❖ Terminate the pregnancy

As a consultant, you send two basic messages:

1. No matter what happens, or what you decide, I will always love you.

2. You have some tough decisions to make—painful decisions. Because I love you, I hurt for you. I will be here for you, but I can't take the pain away, and I can't make the decisions for you. I'll be happy to help you explore all the options, if you like.

Exploring Choices

One grandmother-to-be said, "I know in my heart that adoption is the best option for my daughter. But that is very difficult for me because of the pain and grief that would result from losing my newborn grandchild."

❦ *In consulting with your teen, keep in mind your most important goal: To help that child make the decision that is best for her or him.*

Also keep in mind that you want to assist your daughter or son through a difficult situation, but you don't want to rescue her/him, or take responsibility for solving the problem, which would serve only to weaken and disable the very person you want to help.

❦ *When we create dependent adult children, we rob them of the opportunity to provide their own joy.*

It is a common phenomenon of life for grandparents that nothing gives us as warm a feeling as helping our loved ones out of tough spots. But nothing gives us a worse feeling than chronically being expected to pull them out of holes of their own digging. When rescue is expected, the job of helping is reduced and the person being rescued is robbed of independence and the opportunity for self-respect. As a result, we can unwittingly cripple a teen parent with too much help.

Tammy's Two Evenings per Week

Tammy decided to keep her baby, and her parents decided they could live with that decision. Tammy found an apartment to move into a couple of months after Josh was born. After a few weeks, though, she discovered how time-consuming baby-care is without assistance.

"I have no life except work, sleep, and caring for Josh," she told her parents. "I need someone to watch him."

"I know that caring for a baby is a lot of work and very tiring," her mother said, "Who were you thinking of for a baby-sitter?"

Tammy, puzzled, looked at her mother. "Well, you!" she said.

"What are your other thoughts on that?" her mother asked gently.

"I thought you'd take him on weekends so I could see my friends. I can't be expected to be around a kid all the time, you know."

Mom offered to give it some thought and get back to her.

Tammy's parents decided that they would love to care for Josh two evenings per week during the week. They felt this would help their daughter, without crippling her.

Jessica's Support

When 16-year-old Jessica was pregnant, her family, friends and fellow church members did not turn away. Instead, they affirmed her decision to carry her pregnancy to term, gave her several elaborate baby showers, and lavished her with attention. They "oohed" and "ahhed" over the baby when it was born, and went to great lengths to help Jessica, offering both care for the child and financial support. That lasted about a year.

More and more, Jessica found herself alone with the responsibility of caring for her child. She had received a lot of support, and missed it. She wanted more affirmation. Because she needed more attention, Jessica went out and got pregnant again.

The people Jessica spent time with had helped her in the only way they knew, but had never given her the kind of assistance she really needed—the kind of prodding questions that force a teen mother to think for herself, such as: "How are you feeling about this life change? Are you going to be okay once we all go back to our own lives? What are you going to do?"

How much time and money grandparents will provide becomes a crucial issue when a teenage daughter decides to keep her baby and to not marry. Child care and finances are huge concerns she must address. When the pregnancy is revealed, grandparents-to-be can respond in a number of ways:

Response #1: "It's unfair of you to saddle me with a baby."
By making this statement, grandparents assume that caring for the child is a given—that they have no choice in the matter.

Response #2:
"Are you expecting us to take care of your baby?"
This statement takes no stand on the issue. Rather, it leaves the daughter in control of making the decision about who will care for the child.

Response #3:
"I don't want to have to take care of that baby."
While this is expressed as a protest, the way it is phrased can plant a seed in the teen parent's mind that there is room for challenge and debate.

Response #4: "How do you plan to care for this baby?"
This statement places responsibility firmly where it belongs—on the shoulders of the parent. Then grandparents-to-be have only to decide how much assistance they wish to offer.

Relieving Marital Stress

Few family members consider the marital stress caused a set of grandparents who have a pregnant teen at home. Stephanie, who was one of those grandparents, remembers, "My husband wasn't much help at the beginning when we learned our daughter, who was a freshman in college, was pregnant. He was back in school himself and buried himself in his books to wipe the situation out of his mind. I felt very much alone. It was almost as if every time he looked at me, he saw the problem."

Some grandparents wind up arguing about the parenting they themselves did. Bonnie, a young grandmother, said, "I wondered what I did wrong, or what my husband did wrong. Were we too lenient? Too strict? We argued about it and blamed each other at first."

As grandparents adjust to the initial shock, they find there are decisions to be made that need discussion. Grandparents-too-soon may wish to consult with someone outside the family to help them through the multitude of choices before them. The person they choose doesn't have to be a professional. It can be a respected family friend, a church pastor, or counselor.

Whatever decisions are made, there are some important ground rules to keep in mind:

1. Decisions about child care and financial support must be mutually made and agreed upon by both grandparents.

The worst possible scenario is one grandparent helping with finances behind the back of the other. When a lady named Kim had her baby, she still owed her parents money for a college loan they had given her. Kim and her parents agreed that she would work for the family business to pay back the loan. Kim never put in the required hours, but her mother wrote off the loan balance anyway. In addition, she sent Kim $100 in cash every month to keep her afloat. When Kim's father found out, he exploded. What was originally an issue about Kim's responsibilities expanded into multiple issues about trust between spouses, deception, and taking sides.

2. Grandparents need to find a solution that works for both of them and abide by their decision religiously.

When Sharon and Ben's daughter had her baby, Sharon wanted to help out with child care, but her husband was reluctant. Their daughter found a baby-sitting co-op for weekdays, but still needed help on weekends when she worked. Her parents compromised. They would take care of their grandchild on Saturdays, but not Sundays. Further, two Saturdays each month Sharon would baby-sit alone while Ben went golfing.

Ben and Sharon are both happy with the arrangement. Sharon gets to care for her grandson, and Ben gets to golf. "It's my get-out-of-jail-free card," he says. Before Sharon started baby-sitting, he had been reluctant to spend two Saturdays a month on the golf course. Their decision freed him to do something he wanted to do as well as participate in something his wife wanted to do.

3. Grandparents need to consistently state aloud what they are willing to do, in positive terms.

Once grandparents have agreed on how much assistance they are willing to provide, they can ask their son or daughter, "What do you think would be appropriate for our involvement and aid? Do you have any expectations?" A son or daughter may wish no assistance at all, or may want the moon, the sun, and the stars. If discussions have occurred and decisions have been made during the pregnancy, all that's left to do at the time the newborn child appears is to work the agreed-upon plan.

One set of grandparents had already reached a decision about child care in the middle of their daughter's pregnancy. After asking her expectations, they made their decision, and told her their plan.

"We've decided we can help you care for your baby eight hours a week. You can decide when you would like to use those eight hours."

Throughout the rest of her pregnancy, they reminded her, "Just let us know when those eight hours would be most helpful to you."

This statement and reiteration of their plan reinforced what they were willing to do, in positive terms. They did not make unenforceable demands, but offered her Love and Logic-principled choices.

If you and your teenager have decided that you will live together and become a three-generation home, the same contractual decisions must be made as when a divorced son or daughter moves back home. You may want to review those issues in Chapter 7 to help make this transition as smooth as possible.

Support Groups for Grandparents-too-Soon

In Philadelphia, some "grandparents-too-soon" have found assistance in a support group, meeting regularly with other families. The group offers a place where grandparents can express their feelings and provide assistance to each other in the way of emotional and spiritual support, developing open communication between parents and unwed couples or between parents and single women.

The group has been so successful that they have become a resource for other support groups. More information about groups for "grandparents-too-soon" can be obtained by calling or writing:

Villa St. John
Box 219
Downingtown, PA 19335
(215) 269-2600

Available information includes a sample mission statement and guidelines for a support group for parents of pregnant teens.

When we are prepared for dealing with changes that inevitably color our lives, we are better able to resolve potentially devastating circumstances. The feeling of being ready for whatever happens is emotionally and psychologically empowering. When we see that we have choices, we can make decisions based on Love and Logic thinking.

⟐11⟐

Love and Logic
Revisited

*Nobody ever did anything very foolish
except from some strong principle.*
—Lord Melbourne

Grandparenting, by definition, is pretty straightforward. It is the interaction people have with their children's children. Played out in life, however, grandparenting comes in an infinite variety of forms. Grandparents
range in age from their mid-thirties to eighty or more.
They may have one grandchild or dozens. Grandchildren
may live nearby or far away. Grandchildren may be infants
or adults—and their ages keep changing. Grandparents
may need to adjust to divorce in the family, a child's
remarriage, and even the addition of step-grandchildren.
Grandparents may be part of a three-generation home, or
may become, temporarily or permanently, their grandchildren's parents.

There are so many potential grandparenting issues,
it's impossible to deal with every issue in one book. We

couldn't even do that in a set of encyclopedias! It isn't necessary, however, to write down all possible issues, because the beauty of Love and Logic is that you can handle new issues yourself simply by applying Love and Logic principles we've been discussing in the pages of this book. Once you have a fundamental grasp of the principles, you can use them in any situation.

Three Rs, Two Cs, and Two Es

The Love and Logic method can be reduced to a simple mnemonic device to help you remember the basic principles: three Rs, two Cs, and two Es.

THE THREE RS

Drill Sergeant/Helicopter Behavior to Avoid

- ❖ **Ranting** creates hard feelings.
- ❖ **Raving** removes people from real issues.
- ❖ **Rescuing** puts off decision-making.

TWO CS AND TWO ES

Consultant Behavior to Remember

- ❖ **Choices** encourage decision-making.
- ❖ **Consequences** teach necessary lessons.
- ❖ **Enforceable limits** define boundaries.
- ❖ **Empathy** provides comfort and understanding.

What is a Love and Logic Family?

We know some consultant grandparents who are now great-grandparents. When Andrew's great-grandson was born, he said, "Finally, I'm a great-grandfather." His granddaughter glanced at him, kissed his cheek, and said, "No, Grandpa, you're wrong. You've

---

LOVE AND LOGIC TIP 21
Choosing Your Battles Carefully

The secret to establishing control of children's behavior is to concentrate on fighting battles we know we can win.

Some areas of our grandchildren's lives are beyond our control and best avoided. Any grandparent who has pleaded, begged, and done handstands to make a grandchild sing a song or recite a nursery rhyme for friends or relatives already knows about these sorts of control battles. The same is true in the fight to get broccoli eaten. Such battles cannot be won with commands. A child's voice box and esophagus are hers alone to control.

If we're going to fight, we need to choose a battleground on which we can win. While we can't control how much broccoli enters Brenda's stomach, we can control whether or not she stays at the table. We can't control Bruce's junior-high vocabulary, but we can control whether he remains in the living room after he demonstrates his expertise in four-letter words.

When we engage in only those battles we know can help us make a point or teach an important lesson, everyone wins.

---

been a great grandfather for a long, long time!"

"It's awesome to see your children become grand-parents," Andrew says. "It makes you feel old as dirt! You also wonder what sort of grandparents they'll be. Like you? Better? Worse? So far, we've been pleased."

Andrew is part of a four-generation, Love-and-Logic family. What do Love and Logic families do? They take care of themselves and, by doing so, they model healthy behavior for the other generations.

LOVE AND LOGIC FAMILY MEMBERS:

❖ Give up as much control as they can.

❖ Express their feelings with "I-statements."

❖ Construct up front, overt agreements.

Andrew says, "All families have problems. I don't know of a family without them. What's important is not to let a problem become a huge wall." This is a Love and Logic approach, and Andrew models it. He is aware that we learn by watching our parents as well as by listening to what they say.

🍎 *Most of life's important principles are caught, not taught.*

With Love and Logic principles, we believe you, too, will be great grandparents. We wish you the best as you model the principles you want to be learned and enjoyed in succeeding generations.

In the following section, you will find Pearls—practical-advice reminders of what you've just read, along with sample situations to guide you in your own practice of the principles. We rejoice in knowing how our Pearls and tips work for you and hope you will feel free to write the Love and Logic Institute to let us know.

⮞PART TWO⮜

Love & Logic Pearls:
Strategies and Situations
for Specific Issues

The Love & Logic Pearls and What They Give You

The second half of this book consists of forty Love-and-Logic Pearls, which offer practical advice for handling common conflicts a grandparent is likely to encounter with grandchildren, adult children, and/or their own personal thoughts and feelings. These Pearls explore specific problems and give sound, practical advice on how to deal with them. Many of the Pearls contain sample dialogues illustrating how to approach discussion with family members.

It's one thing to read someone's philosophy about how to handle out-of-control behavior, favoritism, special needs, and support during crises, and another to get usable answers and real-life ideas and actions to take when these things actually happen in our lives.

If you have not yet read the first half of this book, we think it's best that you do so before using the Pearls. Their effective use relies on your first having a basic familiarity with the Love and Logic techniques and principles. If you've read the first half of this book, you now have enough foundation to grasp the essence of the principles we feel work best, and you are ready to read and use the Pearls. We wouldn't dream of telling you what to do, and you certainly have our empathy for any consequences you experience for less-than-perfect choices!

Pearl 1

❦

ACHIEVEMENT

THE HISTORY OF PARENTING in this country indicates that parents and grandparents, in their efforts to motivate children to get good grades, have tried numerous methods. Among them, reward, punishment, payment, complaint, and nagging. The success rate for all of these methods is minimal. The reason? These techniques tend to turn the issue of grades into a power struggle. Present any child with a power struggle and what you get from that child, more than anything, is a strong determination to win. It's an unfortunate detail of humankind but, nevertheless, a factual one.

❦ *Winning a power struggle is usually more important to a human being than achievement.*

In a power struggle over grades, an adult is destined to lose. Why? Because the activity at issue occurs inside a child's head, where that child has total control. No adult in history has yet figured out how to control a child's brain waves.

The underlying principle of achievement is that it takes care of itself if a home is running well. If children have responsibilities at home and take care of them, they tend to take care of responsibilities at school. If children treat adults with respect and cooperation at home, they tend to respect and cooperate with their teachers. On the other hand, "silver platter kids," who get everything handed to them without a struggle, expect knowledge to come to them the same way, and, as a result, they are often poor students.

If respect and responsibility are not the norm at home, worrying about school achievement is putting the cart before the horse. If respect and responsibility are present at home, then focus on poor grades becomes necessary. It is also essential to make certain failing grades remain the child's problem, not the adults'.

If grandparents work as part-time or full-time caretakers for their grandchildren, they have hands-on work to do with a child's responsibility and respect. If they are not caretakers, they may wish to recommend to parents a set of Love and Logic audio tapes, "Making Winners Out of Underachievers."

Even grandparents who are not caretakers can provide interaction that will be profitable for their grandchild's school achievement. Here are some suggestions.

1. When a grandchild shows you his or her school papers, focus on the right answers instead of the wrong ones.

Ask your grandchild, "Hey, you got this one right. How did you do that?" Odds are your grandchild won't know. Then you can say, "Well, either you tried hard or you're getting smarter. Which do you think it is?" When your grandchild chooses one of these answers, he or she creates a foundation and belief in an achiever self-concept.

2. Read with your grandchild often.

If your grandchild is already reading, take turns. You read a paragraph or a page, then your grandchild can read one. Savor the words and the pages, and enjoy this time together.

3. Ask your grandchild to teach you something she or he learned in school.

If she or he can't think of something, suggest possibilities. For example, "Teach me something you learned in math." "Did you hear a new story today?" "Did you have a history lesson today—what about?"

4. Show the same amount of love for your grandchild regardless of success in school.

Show sadness, rather than anger, when he or she has trouble in school. Sadness allows the issue of school achievement to remain the child's problem, whereas anger causes your grandchild to be more concerned with your reaction.

Pearl 2

ADULT CHILD BEHAVIOR THAT BOTHERS YOU

ONE WAY TO LET an adult child know a behavior bothers you is to say, "We've been around each other a lot, and I'm wondering if any of the things I do get on your nerves. If they do, I guess I'd really like to know." If your son or daughter brings up an issue or two, you can model a good response to that critique.

Your son or daughter may reciprocate by asking you the same question and open the door to discussing the behavior that bothers you. You might begin with the observation, "I notice you have . . ." You can follow that with an offer. "Would you like to hear my thoughts on that?"

If you are turned down at this point or if your son or daughter listens to your suggestions and rejects them, you have two choices: 1) You can choose to spend less time together because the disturbing behavior is too large a hurdle, or 2) You can choose to adjust and accept. If you choose to adjust, it's a waste of energy to spend time moaning, groaning, and complaining about the situation—to yourself or to anyone else.

Even if your son or daughter doesn't ask you the same question, you've laid a foundation for mentioning the bothersome behavior at a future time.

Pearl 3

ALLIANCES AGAINST PARENTS

GRANDPARENT-GRANDCHILD alliances against parents are common in unhealthy family patterns. Certain families, often matriarchies (those dominated by women), have a family tradition of grandparent-grandchild alliances. Most often this is grandmother-granddaughter against mother, in homes where it is almost unconsciously expected that mother and daughter will not get along.

Each female waits until she is a grandmother to have her "own child." The young mother, rightly or wrongly, is encouraged to feel inadequate and unable to care for her child. This child then becomes the grandmother's child.

❧ *The solution in alliance-against-parent families is to recognize and break the cycle, with professional help, if necessary.*

In a healthy family, all members get along. An alliance against any parent, grandparent, or child models behavior that will be passed on from one generation to the next.

Pearl 4

BROKEN ITEMS:
HOW TO HANDLE

When There's a Prior Agreement

IT'S WISE FOR grandparents and parents to have an agreement about what happens when a grandchild breaks something that belongs to the grandparent. The agreement may be that the parent pays for it or that the grandparent pays for it. The terms are not crucial, but having an agreement is.

When visiting her grandmother's office, four-year-old Sarah was intrigued by the pulse-checking headset attached to a stationary bicycle. Her grandmother Harriet warned her not to play with it, but Sarah couldn't resist. The headset broke.

There was no crisis for Sarah's grandmother. She had discussed possible breakage with Sarah's mom two years ago. When Sarah's mom came, Harriet simply told her that Sarah had broken the headset. The only further discussion necessary was about the model number and the location of a supplier, so Sarah's mom could take care of it.

There was no crisis, no ambiguity, and no hurt feelings. An overt agreement had already been drawn.

As a child gets older expectations about payment for broken items change, and the child assumes more responsibility. We know one 13-year-old who had a garage sale of his toys, games, and bicycle in order to pay for an item he had broken. Looking back, he says, "I learned a crucial lesson about responsibility that day. That garage sale made a man out of me."

When There's No Prior Agreement

Juanita had never discussed possible breakage with her son or grandsons. When they were visiting her one summer afternoon, Juanita reminded them that house rules did not permit throwing a baseball indoors. While she was fixing a snack in the kitchen, her grandsons couldn't resist a couple of indoor tosses as they waited for their lemonade.

Derek missed a catch and shattered a handmade vase Juanita had purchased from a local potter. When the boys' father came to pick them up, Juanita said, "The boys were playing catch in the living room and the ball shattered a vase today. I'm sad about the vase, and I'd really like it replaced. I'd appreciate it if the three of you would have a little visit about that and see what you can come up with."

By suggesting that father and sons discuss the issue, Juanita avoids a three-way tug of war. By requesting that they discuss it and come up with a solution, she offers them some power and some choices.

Pearl 5

❦

BUILDING A FRIENDSHIP WITH YOUR GRANDCHILD

WE BUILD FRIENDSHIPS with people when we do things side-by-side, and when we share interests with them. The same is true for family friendships across the generations.

❦ *We build bonds when we do things with our grandchildren, when we spend time together on activities we enjoy.*

These activities can be work or play—cleaning the garage or playing Scrabble; they can be based on your special interests or those of your grandchild. You will find that you don't have to work hard to build this special friendship. If you find the activities enjoyable—together—the friendship naturally follows. All you have to be is you—with them.

Pearl 6

CONFLICTS WITH GRANDPARENTS

SOMETIMES ADULT CHILDREN and grandchildren can get caught in conflicts between sets of grandparents, particularly over where to spend vacations or holidays such as Christmas. In conflicts like these, children and grandchildren often feel caught in the middle.

In discussing these issues with your adult children, be assertive rather than aggressive. Using "I-statements," talk about where you stand and how you feel about an issue rather than tell your children how they should act and what they should do. It also helps to acknowledge your understanding of their dilemma.

Graciousness is a key word for grandparents. Invoking guilt in order to get a larger portion of the holiday pie may be effective—but only in the short run. Healthy families get together because they want to see each other. They remember that in the past they've had fun and have felt good spending time together. Sick families get together out of obligation or guilt, and fun is never a consideration. Trying to motivate visits through guilt leads to alienation—and eventually causes your piece of pie to become miniscule.

🍎 *Grace is more powerful than guilt.*

Another avenue of resolution might be to talk the conflict over with the other grandparents, providing your children are in agreement. If your kids think it's a bad idea, it well may be—depending on the responsibility and maturity level of your adult child and his or her spouse. If your children have no problem with the idea, have a grandparents-only dinner and use the time to discuss any issue you want to share.

Pearl 7

DEATH OF A GRANDPARENT

A CHILD'S UNDERSTANDING of death varies with age. Children under four years of age understand only that a grandparent is gone. At four to five years of age, they can begin to comprehend that their grandparent is gone and living in another place. Between the ages of six and seven, they begin to ask questions about the hereafter. "When grandpa's soul left, where did it go? Where is it now? What is heaven like?"

One wise grandfather explained his wife's death to his grandchildren in a way they could understand. He pulled out two candles and lit the first one. He said, "This is grandma when she was living. The flame is her life, and the candle is her body.

He used the first candle to light the second. He hid the second candle behind his chair, then blew out the first. Holding that first candle, he said, "This is what we will see when we go to see Grandma. We will see her body without the flame of her life. But we know that hidden away from us in a place we can't see—like the burning candle behind the chair—Grandma still lives."

Grade school children cope with death about as well as the adults in their lives. By eighth or ninth grade, however, they make independent decisions. "Mom is taking this really hard, but I don't feel that bad. I'm glad Grandma isn't suffering any more." Or, "Dad doesn't seem very sad about this, but I feel really awful."

Grandchildren's attendance at a funeral is frequently debated. If younger grandchildren do not attend a funeral, and they wanted to, they may later resent their absence. Wise families discuss attendance with their children, saying, "Everybody who comes will walk past Grandpa's coffin. They will see him resting there, and you will too. Do you think you'll be able to handle that okay?" If the child says yes, he or she should be part of the funeral service. It's easy to give children a sense that they're fragile by shielding them from death. That's too bad, for death, no matter what that child's circumstances, is the only certain thing they will face someday.

Pearl 8

❦

DISTINGUISHING CRISES FROM DIFFICULTIES

DYSFUNCTIONAL PEOPLE tend to see negative events as more awful than they really are; they create crises from difficult situations.

A grandmother called me (Jim) once just as I was ready to catch a plane and said, "Jim, I don't know what to do. We have a crisis over here."

"What is it?" I asked, thinking of suicide and automobile crashes.

"My granddaughter won't speak with her stepfather," she said. I asked how long this had been going on. "Almost two months," she answered.

I told her to call me back when she could say these words and mean them: "Jim, we have an unfortunate situation over here." I told her she was over-reacting and could be of no help in that situation unless she could see it clearly.

She called me after I returned from my trip and was able to redefine the crisis as an unfortunate situation. We began to work on it from there.

Pearl 9

❦

WHEN GRANDPARENTS DIVORCE

IF YOU AND YOUR SPOUSE have decided to divorce, you will help your grandchildren by not treating this event as if it were an end-of-the-world crisis. Children take their cues from adults in their lives and tend to handle stressful events in the same way the adults handle them. Coping well will help them cope well.

When you discuss the issue with a grandchild, the following guidelines may prove helpful.

1. Don't criticize your spouse. Hearing this criticism will inflict unnecessary pain on your grandchild. Simply tell your grandchild that the two of you no longer get along and have decided it would be better to live apart.
2. Reassure your grandchildren that the divorce has nothing to do with them, that both of you will continue to love them as much as you always have, and that they will continue to be able to have contact with both of you.
3. Give your grandchild a chance to ask any questions he or she wishes, and answer them as honestly as you can—without bad-mouthing your spouse.

Pearl 10

EXPECTATIONS

ADULTS HAVE A RIGHT to expect, at a minimum, that children will be pleasant, respectful, and fun to be around. If children are not, there is definitely something wrong. We have met adults who do not have these expectations, and, guess what? The children in their lives do not have these positive qualities.

Children mold themselves to conform to what the adults in their lives expect of them. They also base their behavior on the example set by the adults in their lives.

Grandparents can expect children to treat others only as considerately as they, the children, are treated. If grandparents are whiny and cranky, they can expect whiny and cranky grandchildren. If you are your grandchild's model, that child is learning how to be from you—right now.

At some point, perhaps early in a visit, grandparents can sit down with grandchildren and talk about expectations. This conversation best begins with a question, such as, "What do you think our expectations are here at Grandpa and Grandma's house? What do you think we expect of grandchildren?"

Many grandchildren will provide a suitable list: be nice, don't take things, don't break things, put things away, help with dishes.

Then a grandparent can say, "You're absolutely right. What a smart kid!"

🍎 *When they state the standards themselves, grandchildren do better than when they simply listen to you lay down the law.*

Pearl 11

❦

FINANCIAL SUPPORT FROM GRANDPARENTS

ALTHOUGH GRANDPARENTS can provide financial assistance for adult children and grandchildren in need, you want to be careful not to create a family welfare system that leads to dependence. Remember that total support without effort or contribution by the person receiving help can cripple that person. It can also lead to that person resenting the very hand that feeds him.

When you offer financial assistance or when you are asked for it, remember to talk about it in terms of what you are willing to provide. Describe what will work for you, without feeling that you must offer reasons, rationalizations, or explanations. Providing reasons opens the door for debate, challenge, and resentment. Stating only what you are willing to do keeps that door firmly closed.

What John Was Willing to Do

When the factory where Fred worked closed and he couldn't balance his family budget on unemployment compensation, his father, John, offered to provide grocery money for the next six months and estimated what a grocery bill would average for a family of four.

"I've given your situation some thought," said John, "And that's what I'm willing to do."

"Do you realize, Dad," said Fred, "that I still won't have enough income to cover the house payment?"

"That may be," said John. "Providing grocery money for your family is what works for me."

Fred attacked. "What do you plan to do with all that other extra cash you have lying around?"

"Spend it or save it, I guess," John answered him calmly. "But I'll make sure to have the grocery funds available for you. Thanks for asking."

It took only one conversation with Fred to resolve requests for more funds. John provided Fred with no reasons or rationalizations he could challenge—only with information about what he was willing to do.

Pearl 12

❧

FINANCIAL SUPPORT TO PARENTS

IF GRANDPARENTS HAVE financial needs they are unable to meet and believe financial assistance from their children is appropriate, they need to make their needs known. They need to explain how long they expect their need to last and what their plans are for paying or not paying back.

❧ *When a need is unspoken,*
there is fertile ground for resentment.

Chronically unhappy people often whine, "He/she should have known without my saying so." But that's just not true.

Grandparents also need to realize that, in the twentieth century, their adult children have the option of meeting or not meeting those needs. When adult children come to parents for financial assistance, their parents have the right to say, "Here's what will work for me." Adult children have that same right.

Pearl 13

GIFTS

GIFTS ARE WONDERFUL when they make both the giver and the receiver feel good. In our families, we like to make some of these gifts surprises.

Charlie Learns to Match Funds

I (Jim) once woke my son Charlie up early in the morning and took him to the garage to see a new mountain bike we'd bought for him. There was no special occasion, and he hadn't asked for it. We had seen him admiring them, though, checking the price tags and trying out his friends' mountain bikes when they pedaled over to our house. It was so much fun for us to give him that mountain bike, and equally exciting for him to unexpectedly receive it.

When Charlie asked us for things, we didn't buy them and wake him up to a surprise in the garage. His requests were treated differently. We used the concept of matching funds. We told him we'd be willing to pay twenty, forty, or sixty percent, depending on our decision at the time, just as soon as he could raise the rest of the funding. Working for things he wanted helped Charlie develop into a responsible person who could solve his own problems.

Some grandparents help their grandchildren by finding ways for them to earn money to purchase items they want. Some give their younger grandchildren money earned from collecting aluminum cans if the kids take them to the recycling center themselves. Others pay grandchildren for mowing lawns, washing windows, or helping run garage sales.

Two creative grandparents we know keep a list of "Jobs That Need Doing" on the refrigerator. They let their grandchildren bid for the work. The lowest bid gets the job. We're not sure what those grandparents will do if their grandchildren catch on to the high finances of trusts, monopolies, and price fixing, but we've all agreed it will be interesting to find out!

When grandparents give their grandchildren gifts, they know they are on safe ground if those gifts meet the standards discussed in Chapter 6.

Pearl 14

❦

GRANDPARENTS' RIGHTS

EACH STATE HAS ITS OWN LAW authorizing grandparent visitation under certain circumstances. Since every state statute is different, it is necessary to consult your state law for your specific rights. The American Association of Retired Persons (AARP) provides the following information on grandparents' rights:[17]

❖ Granting grandparent visitation rights is not automatic. State laws give you the right to ask the court to obtain them.

❖ The court decides whether visitation is in the child's best interest.

❖ Only after the court enters its order will you have the "right" to visit your grandchildren.

❖ Some states have informal dispute resolution systems to help settle visitation disputes.

❖ Most state statutes limit petitions to situations involving death or divorce of the parent, but some have adopted broader laws.

❖ Without specific state laws, courts usually won't order grandparent visitation when both parents are alive and still living together.

AARP has a brochure with further information on grandparent visitation rights. It also has a current list of grandparents' rights organizations. These may be requested by writing:

AARP
601 E. Street, NW
Washington, D.C. 20049

Pearl 15

HOUSE RULES

IN GENERAL, the person who pays the rent or owns the home sets the standards of behavior for that space. At home, children live by their parents' house rules. At Grandma and Grandpa's house they adjust to their grandparents' rules.

Such rules vary from family to family, depending on the comfort zone of the people in charge. Some adults expect that at mealtime children will unfold their napkins and place them on their laps. Others do not. Some families allow Nerf balls to be thrown in the playroom; others restrict all ball throwing to outdoors.

Whatever the house rules, it is wise for grandparents to state them in terms of enforceable limits:

"You are welcome to play in the living room as long as you don't endanger the furnishings."

"You are welcome to eat with us as long as your manners

are acceptable and you use language acceptable in this household."

"You are welcome to be around the adults when it's fun for us to be around you."

If children violate house rules, it's time for action. You can say, "It's time to play outdoors now; I'm not having a good time around you." At the Cline home, the instruction for children who have stepped over the bounds of good table manners is, "Honey, take your plate to the dryer." Cline grandchildren know when they hear this that they have overstepped their limits and will finish their meal standing next to their plate, which rests on the laundry room dryer.

Although obeying house rules is the basic principle, some grandparents find themselves compromising when their adult children have more restrictive rules than they do.

One grandmother told us one son and daughter-in-law feel very strongly about limiting their children's TV time to carefully screened videotapes. "When these grandchildren come to visit me, I do not allow them to watch television programs their parents have not approved," she said. "However, when my other grandchildren come, we allow them to watch television shows we are comfortable with."

These grandparents have wisely adapted their house rules to meet the strong needs of their adult children. Naturally, this avoids undermining their family structure. As we've mentioned, children can easily adapt to different house rules in the same way they adapt to different teaching styles in school.

Pearl 16

❦

INCREASING INVOLVEMENT WITH GRANDCHILDREN

WHETHER THEY LIVE across town or across the country, some grandparents would like to see more of their grandchildren. Many of them, however, fail to make their wishes known. They plod through year after year hungry for more contact with grandchildren and never verbalize this to the people who could make a difference.

When you want more involvement with your grandchildren, the first step is to make your wishes known to the people in charge—those kids' parents. But rather than accusing, whining, or making guilt-producing statements, you can be gentle, straightforward, and honest, making your request with "I-statements."

❖ "I'm wondering if it would work out for me to see the kids a little more often. I'd really enjoy that."

❖ "I would love to see Jill and Susan more often than once a year. Is there something we can do about that?"

The response will chart your course of action. Your son or daughter may be surprised and accommodating. "I didn't realize that, Dad. Let's see what we can do." With that response, you're home free.

The response you hear may also be about the inconveniences and difficulties of arranging such time.

◆ "I know, Mom, but we're just so busy with our jobs, and their school and baseball and tennis games. It seems we hardly have time to eat, let alone visit."
◆ "It's tough, Dad, but we just can't afford to travel across the state every month, especially with the doctor bills right now."

If the response indicates difficulties, you may be able to find ways to make contact easier.

◆ "We'd be willing to provide transportation to some of their games if that would help you out. That way we'd see the kids, and you'd have some free time."
◆ "If it's okay with you, we can pay for plane tickets for the kids every few months—or maybe we can meet halfway to spend a weekend together."

❦ *It never hurts to ask, "Is there something I can do that would make you feel better about my spending more time with the kids?"*

Pearl 17

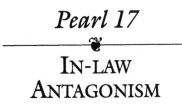

IN-LAW ANTAGONISM

WE DO NOT CHOOSE our sons- and daughters-in-law; our daughters and sons do. Sometimes we are pleased with their choices and sometimes not. Regardless of our feelings, our kids have selected their mates because that person meets a special need in their life. We need to find ways to make peace with their choices. Perhaps these will be helpful to you:

1. Don't criticize your son or daughter-in-law to your child.

The result of criticism is likely to be resentment. After all, you are criticizing their choice of a mate and that reflects badly on their own person as well.

2. Don't fake affection you don't feel.

When you pretend to care, your true feelings ooze from every pore. Affection is something that is not easily faked.

3. Extend to people genuine courtesy and politeness.

If you practice courtesy and politeness in general, all you have to do is extend it to sons- or daughters-in-law, as you would to any stranger to whom you are giving the benefit of the doubt.

4. Take care of yourself by spending less time with an in-law you dislike.

You can be polite without becoming a martyr. You can spend an evening playing golf together, but you don't have to spend a two-week family vacation at a lake together. If your son or daughter appears content and satisfied, there is nothing to do. If, however, your son or daughter appears unhappy in the marriage, you may wish to open the door with a question.

"You seemed really frustrated with Zeke yesterday. Do you want to talk about it?"

If your daughter opens that door and voices her frustrations, you can offer support.

"I'd like to be supportive of you. Tell me if there's any way I can be of assistance to you."

Where this conversation leads depends on where your son or daughter takes it. If at any time he or she closes the door, it's best to let it stay closed.

Pearl 18

INVOLVEMENT IN CHILDREN'S MARITAL ISSUES

WHEN IT COMES TO their children's marriage, grandparents need to follow in the footsteps of the honorable Oracle at Delphi. Like the Oracle, they have been around for a long time, they have much wisdom to impart, but they wait to be consulted. After all, the Oracle did not go sprinting to Athens and Sparta and announce, "Hello, I'm the Oracle, and here is my wisdom on this issue."

If grandparents are really daring, they might ask, "Would you like to hear some of my thoughts and ideas?" Then they can proceed with caution to take two steps. They can make "I-statements," confessing similar tensions in their own marriage, and/or provide information in a supportive way. Period.

🥟 *Oracles don't issue orders, they share wisdom.*

Pearl 19

KEEPING IN TOUCH WITH GRANDCHILDREN

ALTHOUGH NOTHING CAN REPLACE the joy of your grandchild sitting right on your lap or with you at your dinner table, our electronic age has produced some superb second-best substitutes. We'll mention just a few:

1. Faxes and electronic mail

Computer communication can provide the give-and-take of communication without a three-to-five-day wait for mail delivery. Grandpa and Grandma feel closer when grandchildren know they are getting your picture the same day you fax it. The technology is here. If you have access to it, why not use it?

2. Videotapes

The very first gift some grandparents give their adult children is a camcorder. By viewing videotapes, grandparents can share their grandchild's first words, first steps, and first time on the school bus.

One family we know also provides a video record for their children and grandchildren—photographing places the grandparents have lived, taping themselves reminiscing about family history.

3. Telephone

Some grandparents believe in keeping their telephone lines hot in order to maintain a warm relationship with their grandchildren. Their conversations aren't long, just frequent little two- to five- minute visits about the events of the day and week.

4. Cards, letters, and pictures

Some grandparents keep the mail carrier's bag full of pictures of themselves, photos of places they've seen, and notes and cards detailing the things they've done. They may request the same from their grandchildren, without expecting that a letter will always be sent when a letter is received.

Pearl 20

—❦—

LOST CONTACT
WITH GRANDCHILDREN

WHEN PARENTS PREVENT you from making contact with your grandchildren, the best thing you can hope for is that the problem is yours—that your behavior has caused the problem. If it has, then the solution is within your control. You can take action.

Grandparents will want to ask their adult children about the issue, and may want to do this in person. Or, they may wish to write a letter, instead, to prevent an explosive conflict and to give parents time to carefully consider the issues.

In person or on paper, grandparents will want to let parents know that their relationship with their children and grandchildren is important and that they want to repair it. They may ask how they have caused this cutoff from their grandchildren and express their willingness to make amends.

If, however, the problem does not belong to you as a grandparent, then no change in your behavior can bridge the gap. If the problem lies with the parents, grandparents may try several avenues:

1. Try to find a mediator, someone trusted by both grandparents and parents, to assist in resolving the issue.

2. Suggest family counseling to resolve the conflict.

3. Check with the local bar association about your state's laws on grandparent's rights. Some states have laws governing grandparents' visitation rights.

If none of these avenues works, grandparents may find that all they can do is live with the situation and hope that it changes. If the parents permit, grandparents may maintain contact through letters or cards. In their writing, however, they must be careful not to dwell upon their wanting to see their grandchildren and not being able to, since parents may use this as cause to sever the writing connection.

Pearl 21

OUT-OF-CONTROL BEHAVIOR

IF KIDS ARE TRULY OUT OF CONTROL, they can be told to take a hike or go outside. The rule is: You get to be around us when you are gentle and kind. Feel free to come back then. If adults put up with out-of-control behavior, it will multiply and spread. If children refuse to go to their rooms, professional help may be required.

Love and Logic principles dictate that the foundation for all discipline is a child's obedience to the "Basic German Shepherd" rule. That is, the child understands and obeys, "Sit," "Go," "No," and "Stay," when asked politely. If the out-of-control child does not respond to Basic German Shepherd, all other discipline techniques are likely to fail.

You may want to consult our books, *Parenting With Love and Logic,* and *Parenting Teens With Love and Logic.* These books offer some very specific solutions to out-of-control behavior.

Pearl 22

❦

PARENTAL DRUG OR ALCOHOL ABUSE

PARENTAL ABUSE of drugs or alcohol falls into the category of "tough-to-talk-about." Grandparents worry what to say to their grandchildren about it.

❦ *It is essential for grandparents to remember to shift their worry from "What do I say?" to "What do I ask?"*

Once you've asked some initial questions, you can follow your grandchild's lead without worrying about undercutting parents or planting overly critical ideas in a grandchild's mind.

Here's how a conversation might go if a grandmother is concerned about her daughter's drinking and excessive anger that potentially could follow her drinking bouts:

Grandmother: "Susan, sometimes your mom gets really mad at you, and I wonder how you feel about that."
Susan: "I guess I'm a bad kid, and I do bad things."
Grandmother: "Do you sometimes feel your mom gets too mad? Or do you think when she gets mad, it's

about right?" With this kind of question, her grand-
mother gives Susan the option of saying things are fine.
Susan: "Sometimes too mad."
Grandmother: "Why do you thinks she gets too mad?"
Susan: "I think maybe she has a problem."
Grandmother: "You might be right. What do you think
the problem could be?"
Susan: "Sometimes I think she drinks too much."

Once Susan has expressed the problem, she and her
grandmother can explore options together. If, however,
Susan denies having a problem and tells her grandmother she thinks her mother's anger is normal, her
grandmother can say, "I'm happy you feel that way.
Sometimes, seeing things from the outside, I've wondered if you're in a tough situation and feel things are a
little unfair. None of us handles everything exactly right
all the time, and sometimes I wonder about how your
mom handles things. If you ever want to talk about
how things are going, I'm here for you."

The best basic tone for such conversations with a
grandchild is: factual and curious. Grandparents can avoid
implying pity or a terrible situation. Most important in
these conversations is for grandparents to acknowledge
their grandchild's feelings and to transmit hope.

🐾 *You want your grandchildren to know that
making it through a tough situation is always an option.*

Pearl 23

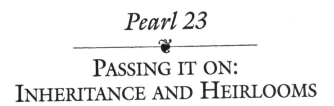

PASSING IT ON:
INHERITANCE AND HEIRLOOMS

SOME GRANDPARENTS PASS INHERITANCE on to their children no matter how poorly their children may be prepared to handle the benefits. Others may want their inheritance to do the most good for the most people. Needless to say, financial planning is absolutely essential if an estate or gift passes the legal limit for free gifting.

The passing on of heirlooms as part of an inheritance can provoke strong reactions. Some people are mortified that families discuss who inherits heirlooms while Grandpa and Grandma are still alive. Other people are mortified when families fail to discuss the subject.

If conflict is a habit in a family system, it may be wise not to even bring up this volatile subject. If a family can handle difficult issues without ripping each other apart, discussion is definitely advisable.

Here are some different ways grandparents handle heirlooms:

❖ Give them away while they are still living.

When my (Foster's) father died, my brother and I went to the courthouse and filed one paper. There was nothing else to do. He had given away everything before his death.

❖ Set up a lottery system.

In some families, the heirs draw lots and the longest straw gets first pick of the heirlooms, and the second longest gets second pick, and so on. They continue through their selections until the heirlooms have been divided.

❖ Designate who is to receive which heirlooms.

Some do it in their wills; others, by labeling the back of a specific picture or item with the name of the person who is to inherit it.

Each of us finds our own appropriate way to pass things on. Since there is not a lot of room in a coffin, and pyramids have gone out of style, the only thing to do is pass it on.

Pearl 24

❦

PLAYING ARBITRATOR BETWEEN PARENT AND CHILD

PLAYING ARBITRATOR IS A RISKY ROLE, because both sides can end up angry with the person in the middle. Be warned!

Arbitrate only if asked to do so by parents. If you are asked, it's best to set up specific guidelines about the issue you will arbitrate, the place you will arbitrate, and the expected duration of the arbitration. You don't want this to evolve into long-term duty.

If your daughter asks you to discuss 13-year-old Billy's refusal to heed his curfew, you can agree to have a breakfast meeting at Breakfast Nook with him to discuss the issue. You choose a breakfast meeting because this is new territory—you never eat breakfast out together. You want him to know this is an unusual event, and that you don't intend to play arbitrator during your regular times together, like your Saturday fishing outings.

Over breakfast you make clear to Billy that you are together at his mother's request. "Billy, I know your Mom is really bothered by the hours you are keeping. She asked me to talk with you about it. It must be hard for you to be in conflict with her. How do you feel about it?"

Here is a five-step problem-solving approach to help you work through your arbitration:

1. Empathize

"That's a real bummer to want to be out later than your mom wants you to be. Are you angry about it?"

2. Designate who owns the problem.

After Billy has had a chance to vent his feelings, give the ownership of the problem back to him. "What do you think you're going to do about it, Billy?" Often Billy won't know. If not, it's time for step three.

3. Ask for permission to share ideas.

"Billy, would you like to hear what others have tried?" If he says yes, you can suggest a menu of ideas, mixing in some bad ideas with the good.

4. Ask your grandchild to evaluate each idea as you suggest it.

"Some kids try sneaking in and out of their bedroom window so their parents don't know. What do you think of that?" When Billy reminds you his bedroom is on the second story, you try another idea.

5. After you've evaluated options together, if your grandchild hasn't made a selection, you need to be willing to leave without a sense of closure.

"Well, good luck. Hope it works out for you, Billy."

If your grandchild approaches you about a problem he's having with his parent, you can help him solve the problem using the same five-step approach. Empathize, ask him what he's going to do, ask permission to share ideas, evaluate options with him, and wish him the best.

Pearl 25

PLAYING FAVORITES

HAVING A FAVORITE GRANDCHILD and playing favorites are two very distinct issues. Often when parents remarry or adopt children, grandparents may naturally have a warmer spot in their hearts for the children they have known longer. Nevertheless, all children need to be treated alike when it comes to sharing emotions and giving gifts. Giving gifts that are obviously unequal is a common way of playing favorites, such as when one child gets a bicycle and another gets a T-shirt.

When grandparents play favorites, the favorite children are often embarrassed and defensive around the others, who then feel resentful. Parents feel distressed by the way children are treated differently, and their own relationship with grandparents tends to deteriorate. When grandparents play favorites with the grandchildren, everyone loses.

With regard to having a child face consequences for his or her behavior when the other children do not need to face them is not "playing favorites." A child may say, "You like them better." Despite complaints, if a child's behavior requires consequences, those consequences should follow. You can respond, "I'm sorry you believe I like them better, but the fact is they're easier to like at this moment. I hope you can change that."

Pearl 26

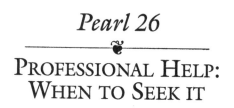

PROFESSIONAL HELP:
WHEN TO SEEK IT

A GOOD RULE OF THUMB to follow when deciding to seek professional help is how long a family has been working on a specific problem. If three months have passed, and the situation has not improved, it's time.

If you are uncertain about how your family is handling an issue, call a school counselor and say, "This is an issue in our family and we're thinking of handling it this way. What input do you have for us?" Many school counselors will be willing to provide advice, and they will be glad you asked. Often community support groups meet at the local community mental health center or at local churches. They, too, can be helpful.

If you begin to realize that professional help is needed, ask people you know for suggestions. When people have been helped by a particular professional, they usually sing that person's praises.

Another way to find a good psychiatrist or psychologist is to ask school and hospital nurses, or school counselors who can recommend competent professionals. Most clergy leaders have good thoughts about community resources and may themselves be good resources.

Keep in mind that seeking professional help is a primary decision and must be made by the person(s) in custody. Grandparents can provide input and assistance for parents, but only if parents ask for help.

Pearl 27

❦

RESISTANCE TO A SHIFT TO OVERT BEHAVIOR

SOMETIMES LOVE AND LOGIC grandparents find that their son or daughter resists their attempt to move from covert to overt interaction.

Stan told his father, "Dad, I don't want to talk about this. We never talked about these kinds of things, and I don't want to start now."

His father answered, "When I was raising you, I wasn't very good at being up front about things. You would think I'd still not be comfortable with it, but lately I've given it a lot of thought and I've decided that being more up front might be better for both of us. We can continue to do it the old family way, or we can experiment with something new and see if it works any better. The old way will always be there to fall back on, so what's to lose with an experiment? We might decide to go back to the old way or we may like the new way better. But with no experiment, we'll never know. Are you willing to try an experiment for just a few weeks?"

Pearl 28

SIBLING RIVALRY

THE NATURAL REACTION for both grandparents and parents is to get involved in other people's fights as little as possible. That includes children's fights. When a dispute rises above your comfort level, your approach can be one of impartial noninvolvement: "Guys, I don't like the noise level I'm hearing. Please take it somewhere else."

❦ *Telling children to take their disagreement somewhere else sends an underlying message that they can handle their disagreement on their own.*

Separating children in disagreement sends them the message that they are unable to resolve their differences, and that you, therefore, have to take action. There are two reasons adults will want to get involved in disagreements among siblings:

1. To protect the life and limb of one of them; and
2. To protect children from psychological or physical abuse done by a disturbed child.

When children fight with each other, it's advisable to not give warnings. Warnings around children's disputes almost always ensure constant low-grade hassles.

A typical Love and Logic grandparent responds to sibling rivalry by making assertive statements:

"Hey guys, will you please go outside and play?"

"Okay, we'll be good," they say, implying they can stay inside.

"Well, I think it's wonderful you're going to be good. I'll see you back inside here in 20 minutes. If you continue to feel good about each other, you're certainly welcome inside the house."

Grandparents can also respond to sibling rivalry with a heart-to-heart talk. You can review heart-to-heart conversations in Chapter 4.

Pearl 29

SPANKING

CORPORAL PUNISHMENT is one of the most controversial and misunderstood family issues. Misunderstanding arises because spanking can be used too much, in the wrong way, at the wrong time, or inconsistently. Because this form of punishment is so easily misused, some professionals have taken the easy way out and have said, "Never spank."

We believe a certain mind-set is necessary. Adults should consider spanking a "big-gun response." In other words, after trying other methods first, it is a last resort. Having it as an available back-up is what makes spanking effective, sometimes without ever using it.

We believe, under the following conditions, spanking is appropriate.

1. On children four years old or younger.
2. Never as a control battle, or it will not be effective.
3. For direct disobedience concerning adult instruction—

come, go, sit, stay. It is never for back-talk, stealing, whining and complaining, or avoiding chores. For these behaviors isolation is effective by itself. If a child refuses to be isolated, then he/she is guilty of direct disobedience.

4. Less and less often with increasing effectiveness. If spankings have no effect and parents find themselves increasing the frequency, it is time to stop.

5. On the rear end—that part of the body that contains the largest muscle mass in the body over the largest, flattest bone in the body through which not one major artery, nerve, or vein runs. It is covered with nerve fibers sensitive to a slap. The derriére is an example of our creator's excellence in design.

6. Administered with an open hand on a rear with absolutely no verbal agonizing on the part of the adult, no comments about having to do it or about the spanking hurting the adult more, and with no verbal scolding.

7. Followed by, "Sometimes stimulation of the rear end stimulates the spinal cord, which stimulates the brain. Thinking and memory improve because the whole nervous system is stimulated. My hope is that your thinking is improving every second."

If adults themselves have been abused, or if they believe that popping a kid on the rear a couple of times is abuse, they are probably psychologically unable to spank and using it will be ineffective for them.

🍃 *Spanking is very different from child abuse. This Pearl is in no way meant to encourage or to give license for child beating.*

Pearl 30

SPECIAL-NEEDS GRANDCHILDREN

ALL PARENTS NEED A BREAK SOMETIMES. Parents of children with special needs may need that break even more. Some grandparents are able to help these parents by providing respite care. Others, for reasons of health or distance, may not be able to do so.

All grandparents, however, can learn to accept their special-needs grandchildren as they are, making space in their extended family and in their hearts. This loving acceptance is a gift without price.

The more special or "off the norm" a grandchild, the more likely are disagreements on care to take place. "Can'ts" get confused with "won'ts."

❦ *Sometimes special-needs children can be very charming to everyone except the people they live with.*

Everyone may feel that others don't really appreciate or understand the situation or the child. Adoptive or foster children's needs for discipline and structure are often not correctly understood by those living outside the home. This group may include grandparents.

In general, the more special the child, the more difficult it may be for all adults to easily accept the other adults' disciplining tools and behavioral expectations.

If grandparents and parents are close and the child is particularly difficult or special, it is sometimes wise for all adults involved with the child to meet with the child's therapist or family physician. When everyone hears the same words straight from the professional's mouth, and when everyone has the same information at the same time, all adults may relate more effectively to the child's needs.

Pearl 31

SPENDING TIME TOGETHER

RITA SPENDS SIX WEEKS with her children and grandchildren each year at the peak of their catering season. She helps out by baking hundreds of homemade cookies, which are a favorite among their customers. After six weeks, she heads home across the country.

"We love each other, but six weeks at a time is about all we can handle. Then it's time to split," she says.

Other families operate by the "Fish and Relatives Principle": Both fish and relatives begin to smell after three days.

The frequency and duration of time that families spend together vary widely. There is no magic bell that dings "enough" when that amount of time is reached. The secret is to know when both parties are enjoying the time they spend together. Healthy families spend time together because they want to.

🐛 *Neurotic families spend time together because they believe they have to and feel guilty if they don't.*

Pearl 32

❦

SPOILING

A SPOILED CHILD is one who sees himself at the center of the universe. He wants his desires met, and expects that they will be, immediately and without effort on his part. When he says, "Jump!" he wants the adults in his life to ask, "How high?" Most people who are spoiling a child do not realize they're doing it. They see themselves taking necessary steps to keep a child content and under control. Worse yet,. they attempt to avoid hurting a child's self-image when in fact they are destroying it.

It's difficult to spoil a ch'ld under nine months of age. After that age is reached. however, it's important for the adults in a child's life to remember to take care of themselves in the presence of that child, so that the child learns that taking care of oneself is not only acceptable, but the right thing to do.

A child can be spoiled all too easily. Here are ways people do it every day:

1. Give the child so much of their time, energy, and/or money that the child comes to expect these gifts as things owed him or her. The child comes to demand them. Buying a gift for a grandchild each time you see him because you know he or she will ask is a definite nudge toward spoiling.

2. Rush in and solve problems for a child whenever he or she runs into a tight spot. Finding the shoes a child misplaced so he can go to a friend's house may already be pointing him toward expecting too much of the adults in his world.

3. Ignore and downplay misbehavior. Allowing a four-year-old to kick a guest without consequences is to spoil her.

Grandparents can limit their gifts so that grandchildren feel surprised and grateful rather than entitled. They can serve as consultants while children hunt for their own shoes by asking, "Where did you leave them?" "Have you checked under the couch?"

Grandparents can provide consequences for the child who kicks a guest, asking her to spend time alone in her bedroom instead of in the presence of adults.

With these behaviors grandparents can help grandchildren mature and ripen without spoiling them rotten.

Pearl 33

STEALING

GRANDPARENTS SHOULD SEND their grandchildren a clear message with no equivocation: Stealing from me, or from anyone, is absolutely unacceptable and will not be tolerated.

When their remarried son and his stepchildren moved in, Jenny and Joe found that nickels and dimes mysteriously vanished. Although they informed their son and explained their position to their grandchildren, coins and other items continued to disappear. Finally, Jenny and Joe gave their son three-days' notice to find another place to live.

"We would not tolerate stealing," said Joe. "And we knew that if they would steal from us, they would steal from others as well."

Another grandparent, who didn't approve of his teenage grandson visiting because of his theft record, said, "I never felt comfortable when he was around, because I was worried he was casing the joint." He resolved his dilemma by meeting with his grandson on neutral territory—at a restaurant or park—and both of them were comfortable.

If grandparents are supervising a younger child when the child steals from someone else, it's important that the child make restitution. After age five, restitution means more than simply returning the item to the store. It means return of the item, plus consequences for the pain and hassle. We suggest that a grandparent talk to a store manager in advance and indicate that he hopes the store manager has some floors that need sweeping or boxes that need moving.

When a child reaches his teens, grandparents can relay this message: "I will never be an accomplice to theft. If I know of a theft—by anyone—I will call the police. I never intend to be an accessory. Don't take it personally if I report a theft. It's just what I do as a responsible citizen."

Pearl 34

SUICIDE

WHENEVER A CHILD OR ADOLESCENT talks of suicide, he
or she must be taken seriously. It is never a good idea
to brush the comment off. Adults must not worry
about making a child feel worse by allowing him to
vent feelings when he is feeling worried or depressed.
It's better for the child to vent those feelings than to
hold them inside.

Adults can open the conversation with questions
like these:

"Do things sometimes seem pretty black?" "Sometimes does it seem like life isn't worth living?" "I wonder
if sometimes you feel like, 'What's the use?'"

Then they can explore whatever issues the child
leads them into. It's important that an adult's attitude
be one of curiosity and interest rather than pandering
or worry.

It never helps to tell a child, "You shouldn't feel
that way." Or, "God doesn't like thoughts like that."

These comments only instill feelings of guilt in that child's mind.

Neither should an adult ignore the child's state of mind. If the child is depressed—if life seems dark or not worth living—it's important to get professional help. An adult can tell the child, "If I were feeling that way, I would want someone to help me." Ask them if they think another point of view would help.

If grandparents are concerned about possible suicide, they may wish to talk over their approach with a counselor before talking with the child. There are positive and negative ways to deal with any given situation. When grandparents are uncertain which road to take, it is wise to seek professional help.

Pearl 35

❦

SUPPORT DURING CRISES

PEOPLE IN CRISIS, by definition, are not able to think clearly. They rarely know what they need, and when they do know, they don't ask for it.

When your grandchild's family is in crisis, don't offer to help in a vague or general way by saying, "Is there anything I can do to help?" Offer specific help. For example, "Can I take care of the kids for you tonight so you can spend some time with Tom at the hospital?"

In some cases it may be helpful to simply state what you plan to do for them. You can say, "I'd like to bring supper to you tonight. Would 6:00 be okay?" Any lightening of workload and decision-making during a time of crisis can be helpful, if sensitively offered.

A crisis, also by definition, is temporary. Sometimes help that begins in a crisis can continue indefinitely and lead to unhealthy dependence. People in crisis—especially those who tend to be dependent—need to know that your behavior is part of crisis intervention and, therefore, will end. You can say, "You can borrow my car for as long as Jenny is in the hospital."

If crises become more and more frequent you may need to check whether your assistance is making future crises more likely. And you may need to check your definition of crisis. Our definition is part of Pearl 8.

Pearl 36

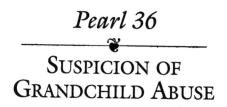

SUSPICION OF GRANDCHILD ABUSE

ABUSE IS OFTEN THE RESULT of parental frustration. Parents don't know what to do and they become hopeless, helpless, and angry, which leads them to abuse their children.

❧ The flat-out, no-exceptions rule for physical and sexual abuse is: Abuse must stop. It cannot be tolerated.

One avenue available to grandparents is to provide parenting information that can help ease frustration and possibly prevent future abuse by giving parents new ways of coping. Grandparents can suggest counseling or parenting classes. They can recommend a parenting book, such as *Parenting with Love and Logic.*

If this avenue does not work, and grandparents are relatively certain abuse is occurring, they should report the suspected abuse to the police or the Department of Social Services in the jurisdiction where the grandchild resides—right away.

Pearl 37

TREATING OLDER SIBLINGS OF A NEWBORN

IN PREPARING an older brother or sister for the birth of a baby, it's wise to be honest. Besides telling them how wonderful the new baby will be, you may also want to mention, "You know, new babies are sometimes not easy. They can be noisy and take a lot of our time."

You might discuss with older siblings an acceptable way for them to tell Mom and Dad when they're feeling left out. Then, instead of feeling neglected, or hurting the baby out of jealousy, they can get the attention they need.

Parents and grandparents, however, can worry too much about an older sibling's response to a newborn, which can actually help create the very jealousy they're afraid of. By saying something as simple as "You won't have to be jealous of the new baby," it is possible to plant the seed for jealousy. By commenting, "Just because the new baby is coming doesn't mean you will be left out," you can give root to jealousy. Constant, overreactive reassurance given to an older sibling can give you an effect that's the opposite of what you want.

In some families, making the older child feel important is hardly an issue. They speculate on what a good
brother or sister the older sibling will be. Grandparents
and parents comment, "This baby is going to feel so
lucky to have a big brother/sister like you." Or, "She's
going to think you're so important that she'll try to do
everything just like you."

If the older sibling acts jealous of the newborn, parents and grandparents can calmly send out vibrations
that say, "Come on, now. Get a grip. I understand
that's how you're feeling, but that kind of behavior
does not help anyone—mostly you."

Pearl 38

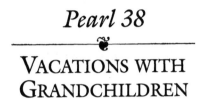

VACATIONS WITH GRANDCHILDREN

CHILDREN BETWEEN six and ten years old are at the ideal age for a trip with grandparents—old enough to be fun for Grandma and Grandpa, and old enough to enjoy it themselves. They are also young enough to not resent being taken from teen activities. At this age they are usually so self-sufficient that they do not have to be watched every moment. Better yet, they can actually be of help.

Before leaving on a trip, wise grandparents go over their itinerary with their grandchildren and tell them what behavior is expected of them. They also ask grandchildren about their expectations.

Some grandparents we know say their best-ever vacation was a Colorado camping trip with their two grandchildren. They camped with an old, fold-down camper, and every evening their grandchildren made a game of trying to beat the previous evening's record for setting up camp. The grandchildren had fun, and the grandparents had assistance.

Children like to know that they are making a contribution to the outing. They can be responsible for their own luggage, help with map reading, and watch for road signs. A child who feels useful to loving adults is a child contributing to his or her positive self-image.

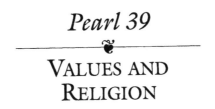

Pearl 39

VALUES AND RELIGION

THE FAMILY IS THE CONVEYOR of religion and values, passing a heritage from one generation to the next. Our children and grandchildren adopt the values we live more than those to which we simply pay lip service. As we've said before, values are caught, not taught. We can help our grandchildren catch our value systems in three ways.

1. Tell our grandchildren where we stand rather than where they should stand.
2. Live our values and be models for our grandchildren.
3. Set up situations in which children "eavesdrop" on us as we make decisions based on our values.

Telling Our Grandchildren Where We Stand

During his granddaughter's weekend visit, Robert told her, "We worship in church every Sunday morning. It helps us know God better, and knowing him is important to Grandma and me.

Becoming Models for Our Grandchildren

Henry and Joan keep a dictionary and a set of ency-clopedias handy. If they don't know the meaning of a word or don't recognize an event or name, they open their reference books. Their grandchildren have seen them do this regularly.

Letting Children Eavesdrop on Our Values

As his grandmother set a bag of groceries on the kitchen counter, Bobby "overheard" her tell his grand-father, "I almost got free groceries. The clerk gave me a ten dollar bill instead of a one for change. She was real-ly grateful when I told her about her mistake. I feel good about it, too."

❦ *Sometimes eavesdropping can provide a more powerful lesson in honesty than any lecture.*

Pearl 40

YOU KNOW YOU WILL NOT LIVE LONG

DISCUSSING DEATH with grandchildren is like discussing the birds and the bees with your children. They send you signals when they are ready for it. You may tell a grandchild, "You know I won't always be around," and factually discuss your illness with her. You may ask if she has any questions. You will get a sense of where she wants to go with the discussion. Or you might open it by saying, "You know, death is the only thing we have a whole lifetime to prepare for." Ask your grandchild what his or her ideas are about death.

After a grandchild reaches his or her teens, some grandparents find that they want to discuss with their grandchild their hopes and concerns for the grandchild's future, as well as issues they would like their grandchild to think about in the future.

Sometimes the best gift we can give the living is the dignity and thoughtfulness with which we die. Difficulty facing your own death or that of a loved one is certainly understandable.

❦ *You cannot help a child cope more effectively than you yourself cope.*

If you're having difficulty dealing with the issue of death, our advice is to let another adult help the child understand his or her feelings rather than try to do it yourself.

Endnotes

Introduction
[1]*Grandparent: Redefining the Role.* Modern Maturity, December 1990–January 1991, 31.
[2]Roberto, Karen A., and Johanna Stroes. *Grandchildren and Grandparents: Roles, Influences, and Relationships.* International Journal of Aging and Human Development 34(3) (1992):227.
[3]Cherline, Andrew J., and Frank F. Furstenberg, Jr. *The New American Grandparent: A Place in the Family, A Life Apart.* New York: Basic Books, Inc., 1986, p. 190.

Chapter 3
[4]Schlosberg, Jeremy. *Grandparents,* American Demographics, July 1990, 33.
[5]Schlosberg, Jeremy. *Grandparents,* American Demographics, July 1990, 33.
[6]Schlosberg, Jeremy. *Grandparents,* American Demographics, July 1990, 33.
[7]Fintushel, Noelle. *The Grandparent Bond: Why Kids Need It,* Parents, August 01,1993, v 68, n 8, 160.
[8]Elkind, David. *The Joys that Grandparents Bring,* Parents, Sept. 01, 1990, v 65, n 9, p. 169.
[9]Neugarten, Berniece L., and Karol K. Wesinstein. *The Changing American Grandparent,* Journal of Marriage and the Family (May 1964):199.
[10] Bartocci, Barbara. *Grandparenting: A Parent's Second Chance,* The Catholic Digest, December 1989, condensed from Kansas City Times.
[11]Neugarten, Berniece L., and Karol K. Wesinstein. *The Changing American Grandparent,* Journal of Marriage and the Family (May 1964):199.
[12]Neugarten, Berniece L., and Karol K. Wesinstein. *The Changing American Grandparent,* Journal of Marriage and the Family (May 1964):199.

Chapter 4
[13]Hein, Piet. *Grooks,* Garden City, NY: Doubleday & Company, Inc. 1969.

Chapter 9
[14] Breslin, Catherine. *Grandparents Who Become Mom and Dad,* Woman's Day, May 12, 1992, p. 40.
[15]Jendrek, Margaret Platt. *Grandparents Who Parent Their Grandchildren: Effects on Lifestyle,* Journal of Marriage and the Family, 55, August 1993, pp. 609–621.
[16]Fron, Mary A., R. N., President, ROCKING, Niles, Michigan, personal communication.

Love & Logic Pearls
[17]Q&A For Grandparents: Questions & Answers About Your Visitation Rights and How to Obtain Them. Washington, D. C.: American Association of Retired Persons, Legal Counsel for the Elderly.

Index

About the Authors

JIM FAY, with over 30 years' experience in education, is nationally recognized as a consultant in behavior management and is one of America's most sought-after presenters on parenting and school discipline. He puts theory into practice, demonstrating the joys and effectiveness of implementing a nonpunitive, consequential home and school environment. Jim teaches seminars and workshops for educators and parents throughout the United States and is the author of over 90 books, tapes, and articles on parenting and positive discipline. His humorous style and charisma have made him a favorite personality on hundreds of radio and television talk shows.

FOSTER W. CLINE, M.D. is an internationally acclaimed adult and child psychiatrist, author, consultant and speaker. He is well recognized for his theories of child development and has received wide acclaim for his effective treatment of severely emotionally disturbed children. Foster is known for helping parents and children with practical techniques that have immediate results. Such practical and immediate help, coupled with his dynamic presentation style, has placed him in high demand as a speaker. His delightful speaking style has been enjoyed by parents, educators, and therapists throughout the United States, Australia, New Zealand, Mexico, and Europe.

Jim and Foster's "Love and Logic" philosophy has revolutionized the way teachers, parents, and professionals work with children. Each has the ability to share his ideas and expertise in a way that enables individuals immediately to envision themselves as more successful with young people. Jim and Foster are co-founders of the Love and Logic Institute, Inc., of Golden, Colorado, which carries an extensive line of Love and Logic support and training materials. They are co-authors of the best-selling books, *Parenting With Love and Logic* and *Parenting Teens With Love and Logic,* recognized by experts as the most practical books on parenting ever written.

Other Books from The Love and Logic Press*

❖ *Helicopters, Drill Sergeants and Consultants: Parenting styles and the messages they send*—Jim Fay
Each parenting style sends a powerful message to a child about what he or she is, or is not, capable of. Jim Fay, in his always humorous, storyteller fashion, helps parents identify their style while offering practical, stress-free techniques for becoming a consultant parent.

Paperback book, 112 pages w/illustrations
ISBN 0-944634-03-6
$7.95

❖ *I've Got What It Takes*—Jim Fay
Self-concept—it's talked about all the time. But what constitutes a high self-concept, and how do parents go about helping their children develop one?

Parenting expert Jim Fay has turned self-concept into a science based on one simple equation. This captivating little book shows parents how to raise children who feel good about themselves and have "what it takes."

Paperback book, 112 pages w/illustrations
ISBN 0-944634-01-X
$7.95

❖ *Tickets to Success*—Jim Fay

Jim Fay takes a humorous, yet practical look at how parents can help their children become independent and responsible. Through lighthearted, real-life examples, Jim shares techniques parents can use to help their children improve their problem-solving skills and develop into wise decision-makers, ready to tackle the real world.

Paperback book, 112 pages w/illustrations
ISBN 0-944634-02-8
$7.95

❖ *Uncontrollable kids: from Heartbreak to Hope*
—Foster W. Cline, M.D.

"More and more American children are damaged early in life and cannot form the relationships necessary to heal themselves. The cost to America as these children become adults and as they produce children of their own—often as damaged as their parents—is beyond estimation."

Internationally renowned adult and child psychiatrist, Foster W. Cline, M.D., takes a hard-hitting look at society's role in creating uncontrollable, unreachable young people. Foster's no-nonsense views on the hard measures we must take to achieve a solution to this far-reaching problem are guaranteed to stir controversy.

Hardcover book, 288 pages   *Available at your
ISBN 0-944634-19-2   local bookstore,
$21.95   or by calling 1-800-338-4065*

For a catalog of additional Love and Logic books,
audiotapes and videotapes, or information on classes
and seminars, call the Love and Logic Institute at:
1-800-338-4065

The Love and Logic
PRESS, Inc.
2207 Jackson St.
Golden, CO 80401